D0065145

THE SELF-CONFIDENCE TRICK

ALSO BY MARILYN MURRAY WILLISON:

Diary of a Divorced Mother
Time Enough For Love

THE SELF-CONFIDENCE TRICK

How Successful Women Meet Life's Challenges

MARILYN MURRAY WILLISON

WEIDENFELD AND NICOLSON

London

ILLUSTRATION ACKNOWLEDGEMENTS

The photographs in this book come from the author's collection unless otherwise stated:

Pat Booth (*Helmut Koller*); Celia Brayfield (*Lorna Cattell*); Sally Burton (*BBC*); Brenda Dean (*SOGAT*); Elizabeth Emanuel (*John Swannell*); Emma Nicolson (*Daily Telegraph*); Claire Rayner (*Amanda Rayner*); Audrey Slaughter (*Daily Telegraph Syndication*); Fay Weldon (*Camera Press*).

Published in Great Britain by
George Weidenfeld & Nicolson Limited
91 Clapham High Street
London SW4 7TA

ISBN 0 297 79373 X

Photoset by Deltatype Ltd, Ellesmere Port
Printed in Great Britain by
Butler & Tanner Ltd,
Frome and London

Contents

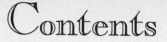

*For Sir David and Lady English, who
made my Fleet Street dream a reality*

Acknowledgements

Some writers are loners by nature and effortlessly produce their books without the help or support of others. I do not count myself among their solitary ranks.

In the course of working on this book I have relied heavily upon my friends and colleagues for suggestions, contacts, criticism and moral support.

I am grateful, therefore, not only to the remarkable women who agreed to let me interview them (see pages 9 to 13), but to the supportive men and women who believed in me – and this book – even when I didn't.

Thank you to my 'network members' – Gillian du Charme, Mary Beth Kerrigan, Heide Kingstone, Fay Ostrom, Frani Pallas, Carrie Rose, Judy Strang, Geraldine Sharpe-Newton, Yvonne de Valera and Lucy Wynne – for keeping me on the right path, journalistically and emotionally.

Thanks to Rod Gilchrist and Giles Neel, for teaching me the delights of having a boss who is also a friend. Thanks to my staff, for keeping my office headaches under control and reminding me of the difference between a crisis and a catastrophe. And thanks to my sons, who didn't let the miles between us lessen their enthusiasm for this project or their love for me.

Introduction

Most survival guides for women are written by learned and scholarly observers – psychologists, sociologists, professors, physicians, etc. – and are directed at urban women who long to have *more* money, romance, excitement and/or career recognition.

Two things make this book different. First, it is written by an author who continues to wrestle with the very problems that this book addresses. And, secondly, it shares the insights and lessons that life – sometimes gently, sometimes brutally – has provided for numerous women of distinction. This is not a how-to book for corporate achievers; instead, it is a look at the inner lessons various women have learned in their quest for fulfilment and self-esteem.

Surviving the challenges of day-to-day life has given every woman her own unique ability to triumph. Personally, I know that stumbling through the challenges strewn in my path has given me a first-hand perspective that could easily be overlooked by more impressive, professionally trained students of the female psyche.

While I have objectively studied how women have structured, coped and triumphed over obstacles as varied as cancer and custody battles in my professional capacity as a journalist on both sides of the Atlantic, I have simultaneously faced several challenges of my own. From death to divorce to transatlantic career changes and recalcitrant children, I've struggled to stay attuned to life-skill techniques that work – as well as those that don't.

Historically, women have been capable of achieving an extraordinary degree of personal growth and fulfilment whether they chose to make the focus of their lives *kinder, kochen und kuche* or the excitement of the market-place. And because that capacity for a life well lived fascinates me, I've spent years tracking the ways women help or hinder their own growth.

Some women appear to have been born with an inbuilt radar system that helps them blithely avoid the pitfalls that trap most of us. And others of us seem to blunder along only to struggle – at great emotional and physical cost – to free ourselves from the very trouble we unknowingly create.

The Self-Confidence Trick is a book that came into being as a result of an after-dinner conversation between friends. My best friend, who has reached the top level of success within her profession, was telling me about some of the unenviable aspects of her life; things were not even remotely wonderful in spite of her so-called 'executive success'. In a cosy Covent Garden bistro we found ourselves looking at our lives through different lenses than we normally used. It seemed that although professionally we were cool, calm and collected, our lives as a whole still left lots to be desired.

My attractive, red-haired friend had recently relocated and restructed her entire life, at the age of forty, in order to enjoy the perks of her new dream job. But in spite of her company car, her generous salary, her entrée to the Royals and the rich, she still felt uneasy about the direction her life had taken. She admitted that she still felt like a novice at the art of living, even though she was an acknowledged professional in the world of work.

I was equally confused. In my mid-thirties, I found myself homesick for the niceties of my life in Los Angeles, pressured by the demands of a Fleet Street career, and confused about my single-parent mothering skills. Like my friend, I too felt uneasy that my life was as out of control as it had been decades earlier –long before I'd had the 'experience' to expect an easier existence.

My friend and I, as the evening wore on, simultaneously reached a conclusion about our otherwise enviable lifestyles. We realized that while our parents, teachers and employers had prepared us well for the rigours of a successful professional life, no one had actually taught us the necessary skills for emotional well being – or growth – that we would need as adult women.

With apparent confidence, we might be able to meet deadlines, manage employees, or organize successful fund-raising events for worthwhile charities. But put us face to face with a troublesome ex-husband, an unhappy bank manager, or a critical family member and the veneer of professional competence disappeared with painful or embarrassing consequences.

We decided that we were both in need of a manual that outlined self-protective behaviour techniques for the various challenging and unwelcome aspects of our lives. Why, we asked, hadn't we been lucky enough to inherit such a survival guide from our mothers?

I was not lucky enough to find *The Self-Confidence Trick* hidden away in my family's dusty attic. Instead, I decided to compile the sort of guidebook that I wish I'd inherited from wiser women who didn't mind sharing their experiences in order to make someone else's life a bit nicer. So, with the help of a wide variety of accomplished women – who graciously agreed to discuss the lessons they learned as they trudged through life – this book slowly came into being.

Meeting and interviewing these women taught me a great deal about them – and about myself. Within my first month of research, their responses to my questions helped dispel one of my own overworked and counterproductive beliefs.

For years I have envisioned myself as being little more than a raw nerve-ending walking through life. If there were a situation ripe for anger or sorrow or anxiety, it seemed that others were teflon-protected from these upsets while I found myself knocked out for the count time and time again.

Meeting famous and accomplished women like the ballerina Dame Margot Fonteyn or the actress Catherine Oxenberg or vocalist Pia Zadora when I interviewed them as a journalist on the *Daily Mail*, and learning of their upsets and hurts, taught me that even the rich, the famous, the beautiful and the accomplished face challenges and disappointments.

Some women (like me) allow life's tests to temporarily destabilize us, while others have learned that attitude can dilute – or dominate – the rough times that life will invariably throw our way.

I am filled with admiration and gratitude for the achieving women who agreed to answer my persistent, prying questions. For while many of us have been busy trying to erect a faultless façade behind which we hide our blunders and bruises, these women agreed to be open about their mistakes – and the effect those mistakes had in their lives. For them to have been so candid, shows just how much they have grown and profited from situations that others of us might have adopted as 'burdens in perpetuity'.

3

Smart women seem to know that we all endure set-backs, but to acknowledge their presence, learn from them, and then proceed on to life's more enjoyable gifts, makes more sense than either wallowing in misery or hiding from fresh challenges out of fear that the same catastrophe will reappear time and time again.

One of this book's important messages is the inestimable value of growth within each woman's life. All too often we think of growth in finite terms. If not reaching a certain height, weight, or age, then earning a degree, a job title, or a name change (as in Mrs vs. Miss).

But if there's anything that life insists on teaching us, it's that the real growth – the genuine process of becoming – is a lifelong process. A woman's growth cannot be defined by finite achievements.

We each have the opportunity to grow – and improve – until death. But because life's evolving lessons offer no diplomas or pay rises or honours, as adults we rarely think of ourselves as 'still growing'.

The good news is that aware women never stop learning how to master the art of living; the bad news is that growth can be very painful.

I recently had lunch with a divorced girlfriend who has been going through a rough spell. First she suffered from a mysterious but life-threatening illness that required two major surgeries and a ten and a half week hospitalization. Then she returned home in the Spring, two stone underweight, to be faced with the accumulated chaos of unpaid bills, a house still decorated for Christmas, and the care and feeding of two teenaged sons. The final straw came when her boss informed her that she was no longer on the company's payroll due to 'budget cutbacks'.

Before my eyes my friend changed from a self-confident, elegant career woman into a frightened, insecure waif. I suggested we go out to lunch to exchange some tea and sympathy and over our meal she shared some of her recent observations.

My friend told me that she was beginning to believe that life was not meant to be the slow upwards 'sunshine spiral' that she had been taught to expect. She had grown up believing that each passing year, in a life well lived, brought bigger and better rewards. But now, in her mid-forties, she was struggling with a protracted series of set-backs that had left her with diminished self-confidence, strength, and optimism. 'When,' she asked me plaintively, 'will things stop being so hard?'

I didn't have an answer when we met for lunch, but I might have one now.

My discussions with, and observations of, women with full lives have taught me that few – if any – manage to escape major challenges. Some women get them spread out over decades while others, like my friend, get them all at once. But challenges do serve a purpose. They visit us to teach lessons that we've otherwise managed to escape along the way. As someone once observed, 'If life is a classroom, then crises are the homework.'

All of life's lessons, of course, need not be unpleasant ones. But it is far more likely that we will emerge as stronger women after surviving an unpleasant situation than an enjoyable one.

My goal is to outline some of the lessons that can help all of us approach life, whatever our age or dream, with a road-map of potential detours and alternative routes to allow us to do what we all need to do: arrive at our chosen life's destination with our peace of mind and our self-esteem intact.

The Self-Confidence Trick cannot guarantee that your individual journey will be without potential hazards, but it can help you reach your goal with an increased awareness of the control you have over your own life.

Learning to like yourself, while at the same time remaining optimistic about life, can be a tall order when faced with challenges. But that process is a healthy by-product of refusing to be a victim. And acknowledging that your life really is your own creation is the difference between maturing gracefully and merely ageing.

1

Self-confidence

The foundation of anyone's life skills has to be self-confidence. Saying that, it's important to remember that the sort of celebrity swagger that cries out 'look at me' reflects far less inner assurance than the quiet belief that gives a woman the courage to say 'I can do that'.

But in today's world, alas, it's easy for us to overlook the 'true grit' of ordinary women's honest achievements in favour of the trivial but splashy media-hyped accomplishments.

Interviewing the contributors to this book allowed me to meet numerous women at the top of their fields, from Royal florist Jane Packer to best-selling author Pat Booth to agony aunt Claire Rayner. And yet none of the twenty women I interviewed admitted to consciously being self-confident. Though their ages spanned several decades, they each admitted that when it came to confidence they were '. . . still working on it'.

And yet . . .

Women without self-confidence couldn't face and survive the challenges life had thrown in these women's way. I found it intriguing to note that the quieter and more reserved the woman, the deeper the sense of inner resolve. Author of the best-selling novel *Pearls*, Celia Brayfield, recounted with great dignity her decision to have her baby even though marriage to its father was out of the question. Actress Jenny Agutter recalled her decision to move to Hollywood on her own and leave her English 'support system' behind. Emma Nicolson, in spite of poor hearing and her family's lack of enthusiasm, ran for Parliament when in her forties. What all these women had in common was the ability to take a risk, even though easier alternatives were available to them. They instinctively recoiled from taking the easy way out.

It's particularly hard to take a chance if you have a history of failure or if you are consumed with trepidation about what tomorrow might bring. But fear not only has a nasty way of restricting our growth, it can actually immobilize us if we're not careful.

Once, when a particularly disastrous love affair left me questioning my ability to do *anything* correctly (particularly judge people's character), I embarked on a rigid confidence-boosting programme. Because I was consumed with worry that anything I might attempt would end badly, it took a few stiff lectures to myself to tackle even the most mundane tasks. Choosing what to wear in the morning was difficult because I no longer felt capable of correctly judging what did – and did not – look good. Preparing a meal was another intimidating choice because I was suddenly unsure of my ability to choose the right recipe, much less follow its directions.

I had the good fortune to realize – before I became a quivering mass of helpless indecision – that drastic measures were needed. No one else was willing or able to boost my sagging ego, so I elected to become my own private (temporary) cheerleader.

When I gave my children a bath or read them a bedtime story, I would compliment myself – out loud – on my stellar mothering skills. When watering my roses I would praise my talent as a gardener. When making my bed in the morning I would tell myself that my linens had never looked better, and on and on and on.

Hearing words of praise, even though they were my own, helped remind me of the vanished sense of capability I'd once had. It took a couple of months of self-administered ego massage before I was able to feel comfortable with even the tiniest challenges or risks. But eventually I returned – with my broken heart well on the mend – to a way of life that ensured I would be tested both by choice and by accident time and time again.

Writer/entertainer Ruby Wax told me that one thing separated women committed to risk from their less adventuresome sisters. 'Some women simply don't have that sense of envy or curiosity or whatever it is that propels us ever onward. They are content with the status quo and with safety. So they don't have to try to make their dreams come true. As far as they are concerned, they are already living their dreams while we are continually working our way towards ours.'

7

Not one of the achieving women I spoke to claimed to have a reservoir of self-confidence. But what they do acknowledge they have is an ongoing sense of quest. They are willing to *try* even though there's no guarantee that they will succeed. And I'm willing to bet that the more they try, the more they are able to accomplish their goal, and, *ipso facto*, add to their growing sense of self-confidence.

Goethe once advised, 'Whatever you can do or dream you can do, begin it. Boldness has genius, power, and magic in it. Begin it now.' Achieving women live that advice.

The women you will meet in *The Self-Confidence Trick* are not terribly different from you or me. They were not born with pools of untapped self-confidence nor were they given a shield to protect them from life's disappointments. What they developed, however, was an inclination towards risk taking and a willingness to test their own abilities.

Jane Packer guilelessly told me that she didn't have a great deal of self-confidence. 'But I do have a restlessness that keeps me eager to find out if I can take the next step. I oftentimes blithely take on a job only to panic later on and berate myself for even attempting to pull it off.' Yet, knowing her tendency to jump first and look later, the entrepreneurial florist – like the nineteen other women included in this book – continues to search for new challenges.

I've met very few women in my day-to-day life who are willing to admit that they have all the self-confidence they'd like. I, on the other hand, fooled myself (as a teenager) into thinking that I exuded self-confidence. Then I spent years wondering why other people couldn't recognize what I perceived to be my strengths. The frustration of feeling chronically underestimated forced me to re-think my so-called self-confidence.

When trying to analyse the qualities that make accomplished women special – in both their private and professional lives – the one quality that surfaces time and time again is their instinct to *do* something. Even when they doubted themselves, their chances of success, or the effect of their chosen endeavour, they found enough inner strength to stop thinking or talking about a particular project and start doing something to achieve their chosen goal.

Here, in alphabetical order, is an introduction to the women you'll meet in this book and to their accomplishments:

JENNY AGUTTER is now thirty-five years old, but knew from the age of eleven that her future lay in the world of acting. She was chosen, at that early age, for the leading role in the Disney film *Ballerina*. Since then she has acted in *Logan's Run*, *Equus*, *The Snow Goose*, *The Eagle Has Landed* and countless other film productions. As a member of the Royal Shakespeare Company she enjoyed stage roles in 'King Lear', 'The Body', and 'Breaking the Silence'; her TV roles include parts in 'Murder She Wrote', 'Silas Marner' and 'Magnum P.I.'. Ms Agutter has also published a volume of photographs and text on her favourite cities (London and Los Angeles) titled *Snap*.

PAT BOOTH grew up over her family's East End eel and pie shop but refused to join the family business, unlike her mother and older sister. Instead she became a model, opened two King's Road boutiques, learned photography, published a book (*Master Photographers*) and went on to write novels. The success of *Sparklers*, *Big Apple* and now *The Sisters* has earned Pat Booth a glamorous life both sides of the Atlantic.

CELIA BRAYFIELD has enjoyed a varied journalistic career. Starting as Shirley Conran's secretary on *The Observer*, she progressed to feature writer at the *Daily Mail*, then film critic for *Over 21*, and television columnist for the *Evening Standard*; she also wrote for the *Daily Express* and *The Times*. In 1985 she published *Glitter: The Truth About Fame* and last year her best-selling novel, *Pearls*, was published; a third book is in the planning stage.

SALLY BURTON used to be best known for being Richard Burton's wife. But she's begun to carve her own identity since his death three years ago. Sally's career began with a job as a secretary for the BBC; with time she was promoted to the production end of filming and met her future husband during the filming of Tony Palmer's film *Wagner*. Emerging from the shadow of widowhood, Ms Burton worked on TV-am's Summer Sunday show last year and has just completed her first novel.

LYNDA CHALKER has been called the Tory Party's Shirley Williams. In spite of her alleged liberalism, she has managed to earn a seat on her Privy Council and to serve as number two in the Foreign and Commonwealth Office. She was educated at Heidelberg and

London universities, earned the Merseyside seat of Wallasey in 1973, and has been an MP for the past fifteen years.

SHIRLEY CONRAN is the ex-wife of Sir Terence Conran, but since her first novel *Lace* was published in 1982 she has enjoyed the pleasures of being a millionaire author in her own right. Her first book, published in 1975, was the highly successful *Superwoman*. Last year saw the publication of another novel, *Savages*; her frank opinions on everything from violence to face-lifts ensures that her name stays in the news.

BRENDA DEAN became a household name during SOGAT's dispute with Rupert Murdoch's newspapers in 1985. Her career began, at the age of sixteen, when she worked as a typist in a Stretford printing firm. In 1959 she became Administration Secretary of the Manchester Branch of SOGAT; in 1971 she was elected Assistant Branch Secretary and in 1976 she was elected Branch Secretary. She became General President of SOGAT in 1983 and was elected General Secretary in 1985.

ELIZABETH EMANUEL attended The Harrow School of Art where she met, and married, her husband and partner, David Emanuel, thirteen years ago. The Princess of Wales chose the Emanuels to design her wedding dress and still favours their designs, most recently for the Royal visit to the Gulf. Elizabeth Emanuel's interests are not limited to couture; an Emanuel shop has opened in Knightsbridge and theatre and opera designs now form an integral part of the business, as do their hosiery, stationery, and accessories lines.

LYNNE FRANKS has a reputation for being the hard-headed force behind the British Fashion Industry's public image. With frizzy hair, teenage clothes, and the face of a harried housewife, it's hard to reconcile her thriving public relations empire with the casual but committed personality who runs it. Married with two children, Lynne Franks acknowledges that people often find her abrasive, but she feels that others are also all too willing to 'let Lynne do it'. She has worked hard for the Labour Party.

LESLIE KENTON served as *Harpers & Queen* Health and Beauty Editor for fourteen years. Her role as a health guru was reinforced when she presented TV programmes based on her research for

Thames, ITV and the BBC. Originally from California (although she has lived in Britain for twenty years) she is the daughter of jazz musician Stan Kenton. In addition to writing for *Cosmopolitan, Vogue, The Sunday Times* and the *Daily Mail*, she has written nine books on various facets of health and beauty.

PRUE LEITH was totally uninterested in food until she was a nineteen-year-old French history student living in France. Unable to get admitted to Maxim's all-male kitchens, she enrolled in the Cordon Bleu School. This led to a job in London cooking lunch for a firm of solicitors. In 1962 she opened an outside catering service cooking dinners for housewives in their homes at £3.00 a time. Now 'Leiths' supplies the English lunches and teas for The Orient Express, is a catering business in the City providing boardroom lunches, as well as a *grande luxe* restaurant in Kensington and a prestigious cooking school. Ms Leith contributes articles to *The Sunday Times, The Daily Telegraph* and the *Sunday Express*; she is also the Cookery Editor for the *Guardian*. She has written nine books on cooking and catering

EMMA NICOLSON's family history is heavily populated with MPs. She proudly recounts that three great grandfathers, one grandfather, three uncles, a number of cousins and one brother-in-law are (or have been) in Parliament. But the family was still surprised when Ms Nicolson, in her forties, won her own seat in the House of Commons. In 1983 she was appointed National Vice-Chairman of the Conservative Party by Mrs Thatcher, with special responsibility for women. She has enjoyed a successful career in the computer field as well as in fund-raising (primarily for Save The Children) in spite of a significant loss of hearing in one ear.

DETTA O'CATHAIN, OBE, was educated at University College, Dublin, where she studied Economics, English and French. Her career began with Aer Lingus but she now serves as Managing Director of Milk Marketing for the Milk Marketing Board. Married, but without children, she currently serves as Non-Executive Director of Tesco and Midland Bank. She is fifty years old.

JANE PACKER is in her late twenties and is best known for her floral designs for the Duke and Duchess of York's wedding two years ago. She owns and operates Jane Packer Floral Design in London's West End and has written a book about flower arranging.

ARABELLA POLLEN combines marriage, motherhood and a successful career as a dress designer. Her days are spent in a cavernous Kensington warehouse where she creates clothes that will dress clients as varied as Woodhouse customers and the Princess of Wales.

LADY PORTER's father founded Tesco's. He gave her two abiding legacies: political activism and the importance of the family. Her public service career began in 1972 when she became an Inner London Justice of the Peace; since 1974 she has served on the Westminster City Council, serving as Leader since 1985.

CLAIRE RAYNER became a nurse in 1954; since then, her medical training has served her well. She has written over seventy books, many covering a broad range of medical subjects from sex education to home nursing. She is currently regarded as one of the country's top 'Agony Aunts' having written long-running columns in the *Sun* and the *Sunday Mirror*. On the day I interviewed her, she and her husband were celebrating their thirtieth wedding anniversary.

AUDREY SLAUGHTER first made a name for herself in journalism when she edited *Honey*, an early 1960s magazine that 'discovered' the hitherto unrecognized teenage market. From there she went on to launch *Over 21* and eventually served as Editor-in-Chief on *Working Woman*. Now returned to newspapers, she worked on the *Independent* before joining the *Sunday Telegraph*'s Sunday supplement. She is married to former editor Charles Wintour.

RUBY WAX grew up in Chicago but moved to England in the 1970s to pursue an acting career. She studied with the Royal Scottish School of Music and Drama and the Royal Shakespeare Company. When she decided that she preferred to experience life on *and* off stage, she began writing. In 1982, she wrote 'For Four Tonight' for Channel Four and she wrote and acted in 'Girls On Top'. Last year she was a columnist for the *London Daily News* and the host of Channel Four's 'Don't Miss Wax'.

FAY WELDON may be best known for her novel *The Life And Loves*

Of A She-Devil. But during her career she has written twelve novels – as well as stage, radio and screenplays – and has a £450,000 advance lined up for her next three books. Soft, blonde and piercingly intelligent, she combines a hard-hitting sense of moral outrage with a fun-loving personality. She is the mother of four sons (whose births spanned two decades) and is married to an antique dealer.

Roots

One simplistic truth that life teaches us all is that where we're headed is inextricably linked – even if through rebellion – to where we've been. For years I fooled myself into believing that, Zeus-like, I had sprung into my present shape and form and substance unaided and uninfluenced by my past. What vanity.

Because I am American, however, that sort of self-defined delusion is not altogether surprising. In the States it is almost a *de rigueur* belief that one must turn one's back on the past in order to succeed in embracing the future.

But a part of my postponed acceptance of adulthood – another thing we Americans try to avoid – has been to accept the roots that (for better or worse) helped make me what I am today. And I'm pleased to report that most of the outstanding women I've interviewed for this book acknowledge that they wouldn't have achieved as much as they did if they hadn't had roots to make them stronger by providing a foundation – either to build on to or to rebel against.

My roots, in retrospect, seem pretty rootless. I never knew my birth parents but had the good fortune, at the age of three, to be adopted by a childless couple in their late forties. They had lost two toddlers to childhood diseases twenty years before I was born and had long since abandoned any dreams of parenthood. But by one of those quirky twists of fate that visit most of us from time to time, my father decided that what he desperately needed to give his life extra meaning was a child. And although he might have preferred a son, it was the talkative brown-eyed little girl that he chose to be his daughter.

My first memory is of returning from what must have been our inaugural shopping spree. If I close my eyes I can hear the rustle of tissue paper, see the shiny patent shoes, and feel the softness of delicate little-girl clothes. The pale-blue, fur-trimmed coat with matching hat and muff convinced me that if I were very good, and very lucky, my entire life would continue to be full of such fortuitous twists and turns. It's been a belief I've cherished, often with little or no reinforcement, for the past three decades.

My mother, who was small and straightforward and, on occasion, severe, threw herself into parenthood with a vengeance. She saw to it that my long hair was perpetually curled, that my clothes were conspicuously cleaned, and that manners, prayers and bedtime stories were never short in supply.

My father, whom I regarded as the most charming man in the world, was less concerned with crinolines and doll carriages. Unlike my mother, he didn't see me as a child; to him I was a chosen companion. Saturdays were reserved for special outings, and once each week, he allowed me to choose which movie the two of us would see. In retrospect I am horrified at the way he and I excluded Mama from our social life; but at the time I only knew that Daddy was 'exciting' and Mama was 'boring'.

Our tiny family did not enjoy what was the typical American lifestyle. Because of my father's work, we were frequently transferred up and down the West Coast of America. And it seemed as if every two years, with predictable regularity, we'd call a new house 'home'.

My father greeted these relocations with zest. He had the ability to envision a better, bigger future, regardless of the location. My mother, however, dreaded the word 'transfer', and grimly she would begin organizing our posessions for yet another move. She made no secret of the fact that she hated the chore of sorting and packing the family's assorted treasures, and she could presciently predict which items would get chipped or scraped or broken. She had an uncanny ability to know which crate would arrive unscathed and which ones wouldn't.

And so it was that I grew up attending a long list of small-town schools scattered throughout Oregon, Arizona and California. While outwardly accepting our nomadic lifestyle, I inwardly longed to live in a big sturdy house that had belonged to one family – mine – for decades. I longed to have a neighbourhood history and I prayed with each move that this time – this time –

would be my last experience as the 'new girl' at school.

By the time I'd reached my late teens, and my umpteenth school, my parents were in their late sixties and in failing health. When I was nineteen my father was battling cancer and my mother was preoccupied with making his last days as comfortable as possible; I, with the naïvety of youth, was looking forward to a future that was guaranteed, I was sure, to have very deep roots indeed.

For by that time I was desperately in love with a young man who represented everything my childhood had lacked. He was solid, and ambitious, and came from a large, tightly knit family. His father had also been subject to many 'transfers' over the years and that gave us a shared dream of a steady, secure life.

We married, attended UCLA together, and started our own family. And when we finally bought our big sturdy home – a typical American colonial house painted white with green shutters – I felt that here, at last, were my roots. Silly, silly me.

Life has taught me that roots are not things. Not houses or jobs or even people. Our true roots are attitudes and beliefs that survive the elements, the economy, catastrophes, or even transfers.

My roots taught me not to be afraid of the new, and once I became an adult I taught myself not to be dismissive of the old. Between them, they have helped me enjoy the good times and survive the bad.

Needless to say, most of the women you will meet in this book grew roots that were independent of the ones they inherited. But the valuable thing about whatever sort of roots we have is that we can take them with us – wherever we go, whatever our dream.

Arabella Pollen, the dress designer, clearly recognizes the differences between what she inherited as a youngster and what she has created for herself as an adult. With the quiet competence that you would expect from this tall, elegant artist she admits that her roots are far from linear.

> I suppose the roots I have inherited are part English and part American because I was brought up as an American, which had quite a big effect on me. I lived in New York when I was a child and I think that has had a lot of effect on my life. But from my parents I suppose I have inherited a very English background and the love of art; my family always had a great interest in the arts.

I am still very close to my family and they still feature strongly in my life. But as an adult I have built a life of my own which is not particularly English, but American and Italian because my husband is Italian, so I have had to try to incorporate the whole lot and make it all work together.

He deals in Old Masters so he rather looks down on my work in fashion as being the other end of the art scale. He is totally involved in the 'art world' and here I am in the rag trade! On the whole, however, he is very good about my work, which I never admit to him but still I am very appreciative. He helps me to keep an eye focused on the importance of my family which helps me avoid giving them second place otherwise.

Both my parents are English but my mother was brought up in South Africa so in effect I have been working on trying to incorporate the European side of my husband's family and the English side of my family and also make those work. It takes work to combine them and it's a bit of a juggling act when you compare the European mentality with the English mentality.

Jane Packer became a 'high-profile florist' when she was chosen to decorate Westminster Abbey for Sarah Ferguson's marriage to Prince Andrew. In person, she comes across as a young, cheerful, highly competent career girl.

If you didn't read the newspaper clips regarding Jane Packer Floral Design it might never occur to you that this earnest, smiling woman created the floral 'coup' of the year with her flowers for the Duke and Duchess of York's wedding.

My childhood and my life until I left home was very secure, very safe. I grew up in a small town in Essex. Really the only things that my parents ever wanted for me was to be married, have children and have a happy life – never what I am doing now. They're really pleased for me. They are very proud – I think their friends must be bored to tears hearing about everything I am doing. My parents have been very supportive emotionally but financially, they couldn't be. They are just not in the position, so I was never lucky enough to be given an open cheque – 'There you are, off you go, start up your little business.' It was never like that. I supposed where it did help me was in being very down to earth. You just didn't have tantrums or flit around like a prima donna – you just got on and did what you had to do.

Now my life is totally different from what it would have been had I stayed in that small town – it is completely different to home. I am the kind of person who needs to do new things all the time and go to new places and meet new people. That is what I like and if at work I have had a quiet week, instead of thinking, 'Oh this is good, at last I have got time to have a rest,' I am like a cat on a hot tin roof.

The school and everything that I went to as a child didn't encourage you to have a career at all. It was a very industrial area and that's all you could really expect from life.

Sometimes I am amazed really – I have women coming in to the shop and the idea of carrying the bag of shopping any further than to the car would just kill them. They just couldn't cope with what I think of as ordinary challenges and I find that quite incredible.

Without my roots I wouldn't be doing what I am doing today at all. Even now, speaking about where I grew up, I recall how it was a battle to get where I am.

It would have been so easy to think, 'Why am I putting myself through this, why don't I just get married and have children,' which is – I suppose – what life is all about really. Sometimes I sit and wonder what's right and what's wrong. I know that I am never content and I am beginning to know that I never will be, well, not for long anyway. It's horrible because I wish I just could be happy with my lot.

Hundreds of times, now that I am an adult, I forget to think about whether or not I can do something or not; I just throw myself into it and then think, 'Oh my God, what have I done? What on earth am I doing here? I am never going to be able to manage it,' but then you have to.

I live with my boyfriend and I have been living with him for almost five years now, but he's an enormous help with everything that I do because when I have those horrible times when I think I just can't go on anymore and I'm mumbling about getting out, he's always there saying, 'You can do it.' My parents' attitude would be, 'If you have had enough, then get out,' where he would say, 'Don't be so ridiculous.' We are always having this argument where I'm saying, 'You just think I'm somebody who's got a key in her back and you can just wind me up and push me out the door again.'

17

Public Relations maven Lynne Franks makes no secret of the values she received from her roots.

My strongest roots are the definite drive for achievement. Being a third-generation Jewish immigrant, I still grew up with that immigrant pressure of doing well and obtaining success, despite being a woman in a reasonably chauvinistic male Jewish society. Still, in an ideal world my parents would have liked nothing better than for me to grow up and marry the right, rich young man, a doctor preferably, and have nice, well-balanced, well-rounded Jewish children, and live in the North London suburbs.

In point of fact they are far, far prouder now that I did not take that route. Although all the people I know who did take that route are extremely happy now.

I think my roots also included the sense of responsibility to other people. My parents are very caring people, they're not selfish people, they are healers, not as a profession, they just do it, even when they are tired. They do care a lot about people, they are very kind people, and I hope I have inherited that. I am probably more aware of that now than when I was growing up. So that is what I took from my family roots.

Where I put down my roots was that I had a deep change five years ago. I was living a life of a normal, aggressive, successful, competitive, materialistic woman trying to balance a life of children, marriage and career, with all the other things and being completely out of balance with myself. I'd spent every year since the age of twenty-one, playing hard, but always being involved in work, work, work. I took a few days off to have children, and my priorities were completely wrong. So five years ago when I was dealing with incredible pressure, particularly business pressure, I became a Buddhist. It slowly changes me all the time; it was not just overnight, but it's slowly changing me. Certainly it has been a gradual constant development. My real self comes out, I suppose it is to do with maturity. In fact, the things that I felt were priorities were not. It hasn't meant to say that I have any less drive or ambition because I certainly do, but I am much more balanced.

I care much more about people, personal happiness and the ability to give other people something that I had myself. My basic asset anyway is energy, I have tremendous energy and it motivates other people and I know it does because I am always told it. Not physical energy. So that was a difference.

Five years ago, I went from 'grab what I can' to 'give what I can', and today, at thirty-nine years old, I am happy. If my life had not changed, I would have been divorced by now, I would have been insecure, I would have lost my confidence, I would have wondered, 'Yes, I have got all these smart things, but what have I really got,' and I am not like that now because I have found my spirituality.

Journalist and author Celia Brayfield feels that her roots propelled her into the success she enjoys today. A tall, serene woman, she almost shudders invisibly when describing her young years.

I inherited what I refer to as British, petty bourgeois, right-wing roots. My father was a dentist, my mother was a housekeeper. She was sent into domestic service when she was thirteen years old by her stepmother and she met my father when she was his housekeeper. From that I received a great grounding as woman as a domestic. My mother is terribly shy, to the point of being reclusive. Cooking and taking care of the home were really all she knew, all that she rewarded me for. She was quite unable to contemplate the idea of a woman having a life outside of the home. However, you may find in research somewhere that there was a study somewhere about women whose mothers had been uninterested in housework; I think it was a common factor among unsuccessful women, and curiously, perhaps because my mother was a professional domestic worker, she was absolutely uninterested in housework. She had a cleaning lady to clean the house, and when that cleaning lady died (when I was twelve years old), she did less than the minimum in the house. To be honest, it was embarrassing to bring people there. It looked like a set from a theatre. There was five years' worth of old newspapers waiting to be thrown out.

My father's attitude was no help. He was born in 1895, so for the first six years of his life was a Victorian; he was a very gregarious and sociable man, the life and soul of any party. I think it was a trial for him to be married to a woman like my mother, so his life was completely away from the home. Because of that he was unable to be involved in the running of the home in anything but the most authoritarian and ruthless way.

I remember that many of the houses in Britain were awarded war damage compensation after the Second World War. It took years for this to be awarded and when the war damage money came in, my parents decided to redecorate the house and my mother wanted a pale blue kitchen. The only interest I ever remember my father taking in the home is saying, 'Brown is the colour for kitchens, the kitchen will be brown.'

I was the eldest of two sisters and because of that and my mother's shyness, I was taken out by my father as his escort once I was old enough. He would occasionally take me to formal dinners, which was actually a terrible trial, but something that a lot of girls didn't have. We had a very restricted social life as children because my mother didn't socialize. I was a fat child and the first word I heard when I was five years old and went to school was 'fatty' and that stayed with me for years. I had a lot of difficulty in feeling feminine, experiencing myself as a success-ful woman once I got on to dating and parties. I couldn't say I was the girl who was never asked to dance, because I was the girl who was never asked to attend the dance in the first place. I think I went to one party during my teenage years.

I dealt with it by withdrawing completely into books, reading everything. I obsessively read practically the entire body of Russian literature as kept by the Brent County Library. I had nowhere else to go and I just read. I also wrote quite a lot as a small child. I used to write a lot to entertain the girls at school. There was a soap opera that was as popular then as 'Dallas' is today, and for a long time I made myself very popular by rewriting it every week with one of my friends as the heroine.

I basically rejected everything that my family stood for from the bottom up. This started when I was thirteen and got worse. My parents were xenophobic, chauvinistic in the old-fashioned sense that I think Anglo-Saxons are. In my book *Pearls* I have the mother refer to the Jews as the scum of the ghettos of Europe; that is what my father thought about our next-door neighbours. We lived close to a synagogue and ours was a completely Jewish street and I naturally became a committed liberal. I barely missed becoming a communist. It's probably only because I couldn't find where to join the party, otherwise I probably would have become one.

I was completely fascinated by left-wing politics and by any culture other than my own, but particularly with Russian. I was

romantically in love with Russia and with the ballet. I was taken
to a ballet by a friend's parent when I was about fourteen and I
adored it instantly. The first ballet I went to I couldn't
understand for the life of me but I loved it, and in 1962 Rudolf
Nureyev defected and became my greatest, all-time teenage
crush. His autobiography was part of my artistic education. He
brought out a book about his experiences in Russia and every
author he mentioned, every composer he mentioned I just went
for. I was very grateful for that because I came from a
background in which art was something to spit on, in which art
was automatically worthless. My father told me many, many
times that art is for worthless people. One of his dental patients
was David Hockney and all he could say about him was that he
dyed his hair.

Obviously, Celia Brayfield feels that by living a creative, slightly
Bohemian lifestyle she has accomplished the goal of creating a life
free of her childhood restraints.

The ethereal actress Jenny Agutter, on the other hand, has
incorporated the advantages of a 'rootless' childhood into a
portable security blanket that has helped sustain her in a career rife
with insecurity.

My family didn't have roots, which is rather peculiar. Both my
parents themselves left home when they were quite young; my
mother left at seventeen to join the WAFS and my father left to
join the army. They both left their families and got married in
Egypt. Consequently, they were on the move. My first memory
is Singapore where my father was in the army, and we left there
when I was three. Then my father left the army and we went to
Cyprus. I think every three years we moved from one place to
another – very nomadic. Consequently I have no real sense of
settling anywhere. The only consistent thing in my life, really,
was my boarding school, which I went to with a certain amount
of joy because my brother was going to boarding school and it
seemed exactly like something out of one of those comics.

There was no trepidation or worries about it at all. There was
Cyprus to go back to and oddly enough with all the moving there
was a lot of security with the family, and I just believed that as
long as they were there that was all that mattered. At school I
sometimes envied the girls who had lived in one place, who had

those homes and those set-ups where they just remained in one place all the time. I guess it gives one a different sense of things, although as far as my life's concerned that feeling of being able to move on has been a help because my life has consisted of that. Maybe I would not have lived this life if I had not been used to travelling. Security had nothing to do with place; it had to do with being able to settle somewhere and find what you might enjoy. Consequently, I have never found that I have missed places when I am away. It can sometimes be bad because I don't have a huge desire to settle down.

Security is something that I was given very early on. Fortunately from very early in my life I was given support in everything that I did by the family, which is wonderful. I never had to fight – the only thing that is against that (in a funny way) is that some people have fought to do what they want to do and therefore, it feeds their ambitious side much more, because they've had to struggle to get somewhere, whereas I had so much support. When parents say, 'You want to do this, fine,' it gives you a different type of strength; it gives you a comfort within yourself because there's no one to hold you back.

We didn't really have family arguments about things, but everything had to be ironed out and whatever was done, was supported. In terms of going into film, I have discovered since that it caused a lot of worry to my parents, which I never really thought about at the time. Obviously they were worried about my education and what would happen – would I suffer because of it if I didn't earn a living? But they asked me when I was about fourteen or fifteen whether I should still be carrying on with the schoolwork.

I think in their place, I might tend to be much more, 'You will do your schoolwork and that will be it,' but I think they were probably quite right about what they said. They felt that if I wanted to and that was going to be my work, and I could see it was the way I was going, then they would be behind that. I told my parents at that time that if there was the opportunity to work in film that I wanted to do that rather than worry too much about the 'O' Levels and 'A' Levels and then go back to drama school, which in retrospect is just the way my life went. If I had done something different, my life would probably have gone a different way but what I did have was support and confidence and it made me get into film and then go into theatre somewhat later. But my roots ensured that I never felt that there wouldn't be someone supporting me.

Prue Leith, who has become one of England's top caterers, is a straightforward, cheerful woman who combines efficiency with a naturally extroverted personality.

She surprised her family – and herself – by establishing a cooking career that has brought her fame, money and creative reward. But a look at her roots shows that she has never been a stranger to success. Although she is now happily married – and a mother of two children – she admits that when her career was still growing she often thought of herself as a 'freaky, single business lady'.

I think I can see both my parents very clearly in me because my father was a businessman – he worked for a subsidiary of ICI and was a top industrialist – and my mother is an actress. So from my father I got the feel and love of business and organization and the pleasure in business, and I think from my mother, a terrific desire to be appreciated and applauded; catering is a good combination of both – you can get lots of praise if you do it right and it is a good business.

I think my father would be astonished to see me now – he died when I was twenty – because all the time he knew me, I was changing my mind about what I was going to do – I went through all that, 'I'm going to be an actress, I'm going to be a designer, and then drop out, then a French linguist' and so on.

The last thing he thought I would do is run a business. He died before I had even taken up cooking. So that would have been a surprise to him. It is a great astonishment to my mother who has none of these skills and she is not very organized. She must have been as a young woman – I think all women who have lots of children and a career are organized – there were three of us at home, two brothers and myself. She had a very successful theatrical company and a very successful career of her own running her own business. She had to finance the whole theatrical company and everything, so she was extremely organized. She has now got a bit older and has got rather nervous about it – she looks at me and says, 'I don't know how you do it,' and of course she did it herself. If you haven't got a lot to do, the more you think you can't do, but the more you have got to do, the more you can take on.

What the achievers, with their different backgrounds, have shown us is that no matter how seemingly unhelpful or supportive our early roots may have been we are still responsible for creating – out of our past – a present that is capable of nurturing us as adult women. The following chapters address some of the experiences that can either shape or stall an individual's growth.

Love and rejection

My first taste of romantic rejection came, appropriately enough, when I was still a teenager. I had grown into a bookish pubescent schoolgirl who, unlike my friends, wasn't interested in the campus sports heroes. At that time in our Californian suburb, boys were neatly divided into 'Jocks' (football, baseball, or basketball heroes) or surfer types.

By the age of fifteen I was deeply into my own world of daydreams about an imaginary pipe-smoking author who would sweep me off my feet and transport me to his Manhattan penthouse. Together, in my fantasy, we would read the classics in front of a glowing fireplace and exchange witty *bons mots*. (Talk about an over-active imagination!)

Fifteen is, of course, an impressionable age. And the boy to whom I chose to transfer these fantasies was a student at a nearby high school who wore glasses, read a lot of books and had no interest whatsoever in sports.

I don't remember how I met Steve Goldwater, but I do remember being enthralled by the fact that he was a distant relative of the Presidential candidate Barry Goldwater, and by the fact that, in a few months time he would be a university man while I would still just be a high school kid. My continued preference for 'older men' surely dates from that ill-fated infatuation.

We exchanged poems, went to the high school prom, and enjoyed the standard American 'double-date' scenario – four teenagers, a movie and hamburgers afterwards. There were long, daily telephone conversations and I breathlessly confided to my best friend more than she could ever have wanted to know about what Steve wore or ate or said.

And then, suddenly, Steve's phone calls stopped. There were

no more Saturday night double dates and nothing at all to relive with my friend.

I received condolences over the fact that I'd been 'dropped' and efforts were made to cheer me up with every cliché known to jilted lovers. ('You're better off without him'; 'There's plenty of fish in the sea'; 'The course of true love,' etc., etc., etc.)

Efforts to reassure me, alas, didn't help because I had un-wittingly discovered one of love's hidden truths: the pain of waiting for affection to arrive is miniscule compared with the pain of its loss after it has departed.

I never saw Steve Goldwater again. And to this day I have no idea why the phone calls and the double dates and the poems stopped. But his romantic rejection taught me a few lessons that – even in their present threadbare state – have helped me cope with other goodbyes from men I hoped would cherish me forever.

Perhaps the most valuable insight into someone's goodbye is the realization that love makes us hyper-sensitive – both to its good and bad effects. As a naïve teenager – and even as a somewhat stubbornly naïve adult – I used to believe that love only brought happiness into our lives. But I now know that with its delivery of happiness it also brings a vulnerability – as in 'Will he still care when he discovers the real me?' And that extra sensitivity can wound even the strongest ego.

If I had been wise during my times of rejection, I would have forced myself to acknowledge that I had not really been loving the person who said goodbye. Instead, I had used him as a focus for my quest for love; there's a big difference between the two.

The people who manage to avoid rejection (those chosen few) are usually those who are smart enough to let go of all expectations. By giving love – instead of needily searching for it in command-performance signs or commitments (or poems) – they learn that love can be more rewarding and less hazardous for both parties.

Eleanor Roosevelt once said that no one can make you feel inferior without your consent. But every time I've been rejected (and Steve Goldwater was simply the first in a long line of goodbyes) I've been convinced that I was truly inferior. Other-wise, I would tell myself, the person I was devoted to would not have chosen to say goodbye. It's easy to fall in love and use that person's emotions to validate our appeal or worth, but the danger is that our value then becomes dependent on feedback from the shifting sands of one individual's opinion. Not a good way to build a lasting foundation of self-esteem . . .

Love – and this is a hard one – also involves the responsibility inherent in giving a person the necessary freedom to say goodbye if they so choose. And that means you can't blame them for 'breaking your heart' or 'using you'. It takes years of experience or loads of wisdom to wish someone well when they no longer want to be a part of your life, but the better you feel about yourself the easier it is to do.

Anger, hurt, or sorrow won't help rebuild your belief in a brighter tomorrow, but quietly believing in our individual 'lovability' will. Too bad it took so many goodbyes to teach me that lesson . . .

Because I spent so many years feeling like a real-life goodbye girl, I was surprised to meet so many women who told me they hadn't experienced romantic rejection.

The novelist Pat Booth expressed her romantic self-protection philosophy very succinctly by explaining that she hadn't had her heart broken because, 'Basically I don't allow myself the luxury of falling in love. I'm very cautious of that; I feel I have got too much to achieve to allow myself that kind of luxury. I am very conscious of marrying *the right* person and I also believe women should marry the right person rather than letting emotions come to the surface too much.'

And journalist Audrey Slaughter shook her head the minute I finished my question. 'No – I wasn't rejected, I just made a mistake with the man. I was the one who pulled away rather than the man.'

Arabella Pollen also acknowledged that there hadn't been anyone who had broken her heart. She told me, 'I have been quite lucky – I have never had myself hurt or my heart really broken. But I have had loads of endless rejections on both business and personal levels. I have experienced the same sort of romantic thing, however, by rejecting someone else, which I think is just as bad. If you care for that person and they are hurt it can be just as painful and I have had that happen much more than the other way.'

Prue Leith also had a brisk, no-nonsense attitude towards the *sturm und drang* of romance. I couldn't picture her throwing herself on the bed in a fit of tears or waiting by the phone for *him* to call. Her response when asked if she'd ever had a broken heart?

> Not really. I have certainly had times when I thought that the chap I was lusting for ought to lust for me a bit harder – but I don't think I had a really seriously painful experience. I just never really fell very deeply in love; and all the time I had my business.
>
> I know it is very boring, conventional wisdom, but I am absolutely certain that – and I do tend to think philosophically –if things go wrong, there is some kind of cosmic good reason for it. Even in ordinary business that happens; if you start off with a contract of a business and it goes bust, there is absolutely no point in going on being hurt by it. You just have to think, 'Well, it was bloody good experience, it wasn't right for me anyway, he would never have done,' – that sort of thing.

Writer and performer Ruby Wax, on the other hand, seemed to me to be a bit vulnerable when it came to romance. In fact, when I asked her if a man she loved had ever rejected her, she admitted that most of them had.

> I have always been rejected by men; it was the parental thing – my dad always said I should get somebody like him. So to rebel, I would always go out with poor guys, artists and stuff. It was a real shock to find out your parents have no judgement even when you love them; that real basic thing doesn't hit so I went out with somebody who really was a genius and my father took one look at him (eight years ago) and said, 'This is a bum, get rid of him.' It must have gone in my brain because I subconsciously drove him mad to make him drop me. My father would do this a lot until I got rid of the guy. I have no regrets because he was a wild man but now he's the most successful person in this country in television media as a writer and comedian. He's made the highest echelon – has racehorses, Rolls-Royces, and all that but my father still isn't impressed because he has no gauge of intelligence. He's an information kind of guy. No matter how love goes, you still think their (your parents') judgement is right though.

Both Jenny Agutter and Jane Packer were able to make use of

their rejection. For the actress it helped teach her what (and who) was really important; for the floral designer, it helped (literally) to broaden her horizons.

Jenny Agutter told me:

I have never been married. Probably the first time I felt I had been rejected by somebody after a relationship – I found it very confusing and I felt very much alone. One of the major discoveries at that time was that I think I made my life too much a part of his because I was quite young – this is 18, 19, 20. Being very young I made my life a part of his as opposed to making my own.

The discovery then was that one has to always maintain – I don't know whether this is protection, but I think it's important – your own friends and your own life. When we broke up I found I didn't know where to turn. I had always understood, particularly at that time, that my family were there to fall back on, so at least I didn't feel like a totally lost person, but I did find it very hard, particularly with a first love, just to get through.

It was almost like losing an arm and it's actually a physical loss so you do need other elements – you really do need your friends to make life seem in proportion. And I had cut myself off. I had one very good girlfriend – I remember going on holiday and one of the things that was enormously helpful was being round someone with a great sense of humour because you either cry and break or else you laugh. It helps if someone can actually start to point out the funny elements of the break up. Since then, when things go wrong, I've actually looked at some of the funny elements and I'm sure that psychiatrists think that it's a way of saving face or just getting over things, but it isn't – it's very helpful. If it's purely awful you do end up breaking. Also at that time I had been at the theatre for a long time and I wanted to get back to film, which is why I went to America when I was twenty-one.

In broader terms of rejection, a lot of my work is rejection because one is constantly going up for roles and for every role that you get, there are several you don't get. People never realize this because it looks as though one is working all the time, but in fact there is an awful lot of things that one is going for and hoping for and one is rejected.

Jane Packer chose to spread her wings after she was rejected, which must have taken a great inner strength because she admits:

It was the most hurtful thing that I had happen to me, when I was very young – you know, a childhood sweetheart. That was awful because I think you feel everything so much. I think anyway, unless you are a truly beautiful, amazing woman, who walks in and heads turn, then you are always going to come across that. You are always going to find disappointments because people don't look to you the way you would like them to. I think you just have to face it really, get out there and forget about it. I know when it happened to me, because I was so young, my escape from it was – I was seventeen and learning to drive at the time – knowing that I had to pass my driver's test because the moment I could drive I could just get out of the small town where I lived.

Then I wouldn't have to bump into him or have anything to do with him ever again. I just really wanted to 'drive' out of it. Is that classed as running away? I don't know. Sometimes when that happens to you, you know that the end of a relationship is for the best.

As Jenny Agutter pointed out, life dishes out more than one variety of rejection. And even if these women did not suffer from 'romance gone wrong', it doesn't mean they escaped suffering altogether. Writer Celia Brayfield told me: 'Rejection is the story of my life. I am very sensitive to rejection. I have really had a huge amount of pain in my life and I think that what I have learned from it is not to be afraid of it. If you are in a situation where you are afraid of rejection, you will more or less create it. You have to psyche yourself up to behave as if it were not going to happen.'

Sally Burton explained that she hadn't had to deal with romantic rejection, but that she did feel rejected when she and husband, Richard, spent six months in California. When people there rejected her, rather than walk away or become angry, she blamed herself. 'I find I would think, "What's wrong with me, tell me, I'll put it right, I promise." '

Ruby Wax didn't limit the subject to romance; she also feels a strong element of rejection from her family back in America. She told me:

I was supposed to have a really upper-middle class Jewish American princess life and get a real wealthy husband, and maybe get into something like the linen trade, which my father suggested up until last year. He has friends in the Golf Club who would help me and I could have been a business woman but not a really successful one, you know, fold the tablecloths and go to the cash register.

So I am really a disappointment all round. There has never been a connection between us, so now it is like the dog has just won a lot of awards at the dog show. It's like they will hold the medals up but don't know from whence they came, so there is no gut reaction to the prize.

Everything I am now, had to be created from scratch because they didn't give me anything except money. They did give me a financial base in the beginning, which I am really grateful for; I am not an idiot.

When I asked Elizabeth Emanuel if she had experienced romantic rejection or if she'd ever had her heart broken she told me: 'Sure, lots of times. But it was when I was younger. I just forgot after a while, time heals, and one goes into the arms of the next one.'

Leslie Kenton looks so bright and cheerful that it's hard to believe that she has felt rejected several times in her life. Speaking with real feeling she told me:

I bleed desperately whenever I feel rejected. I think it's because of my childhood. My mother left within the first two weeks of my birth and went away; I didn't see her for a year and a half. I was left with my grandmother and I think that is the most heartbreaking thing of all for a child because the baby's bond to the mother is absolutely essential. I therefore actually bonded to my grandmother rather than to my mother, then I was taken away from my grandmother again and given back to my mother. In my life, all the people I have *ever* loved have left me.

When I started the research on this chapter I wished that rejection could be eliminated from everyone's life. What good could possibly come from having another human being devalue your unique worth? But now that I've seen how these women used rejection to create new life-coping techniques (Prue Leith's acceptance, Audrey Slaughter's responsibility, Arabella Pollen's compassion, Pat Booth's caution, Jane Packer's growth, etc.) I've learned that even life's most unwelcome visitors can sometimes bring growth-promoting gifts.

Divorce

I have several friends – on both sides of the Atlantic – who enjoy enduring, stable and happy marriages. I, however, have not been so lucky.

There are many reasons I could list to explain my mid-twenties status as a divorcee. My husband and I had certainly married too young, we were probably too uncommunicative, and our dreams were definitely too diverse to ever let us become a solid unit. Instead, we were two self-contained youngsters living together in search of approval and commitment.

By the time we'd had two sons I found myself dreaming of a more rewarding, more affectionate, less critical partner. I don't know what dreams his dissatisfaction gave rise to, but I do know that while I was repressing my yearnings and reminding myself of my good fortune in having a successful husband, two adorable children and a beautiful home, he was falling in love with someone else.

Over the years I've replayed a familiar 'what if' scenario in my mind. I've reminded myself of how unfulfilled I'd be if I were still married to a man whose idea of heaven is live (vs. televised) sporting events. I've told myself that my grey hairs and wrinkles would have appeared anyway even if I hadn't been faced with financial problems and a single mother's worries. And I've congratulated myself on having a more adventuresome and exciting life as an independent woman than I could ever have had as a cossetted and wealthy wife.

But in spite of the logical acceptance of the term divorcee – with all that it implies – a part of me still rebels at the realization that my dream of the perfect storybook life was shattered.

And while I spent close to a decade blaming *him* – and blaming *her* – deep down inside some small part of me knew I was pointing an accusing finger at the wrong person. The individual who was responsible for that hated title 'divorcee' was none other than me.

It's embarrassing to admit that I've behaved badly ever since the father of my children filed for divorce. But since *The Self-Confidence Trick* is a book about honest, adult behaviour, I have to swallow my pride and say I've broken every rule in the book when it comes to post-divorce dignity.

For me, the main culprit was fear. I was afraid that without him my life was destined to deteriorate. Because I couldn't envision – much less believe in – a brighter future, I divided my time between feeling angry that someone else had 'stolen' my imaginary happy future and feeling inadequate to build a decent future for myself and my sons.

Hindsight, of course, is always 20/20. But I now know that if I'd had more confidence and self-esteem I wouldn't have been so shattered at losing my husband.

Now, finally, a decade after our divorce decree, I have matured enough to see my ex-husband and his wife as individuals who are entitled to be happy together. Respecting their worth has helped me improve my own. But letting go of my envy wasn't easy. It took years of hurt and anger and fear before I was able to accept that my life was my responsibility and not my ex-husband's (and certainly not his wife's).

The ironic twist of all my temper tantrums and tears was that the two of them were far too happy and involved in their new life together to take any notice of my self-indulgent behaviour. While I imagined that I was punishing (!) them, I now see – with painful clarity – that the only person I really punished was myself.

While I've known several women who have passionately clung to the hurt of rejection or the sadness of a disrupted life, I've known very few men who have made divorce a lifelong cross to bear. One of my friends, who was the 'other woman' in a highly publicized celebrity divorce, told me that she was sure her husband's ex-wife was enjoying her new-found sense of martyrdom.

'I'm afraid she's become a professional injustice collector,' she told me. 'And if she doesn't stop she'll lose her friends as surely as she lost her husband.' My friend, alas, was absolutely right.

Perhaps because I too was an 'injustice collector' for years, I am more familiar with the pain-propelled cycle of self-destruction than most. And I also know that investing in your storybook vision of what 'should have been' is little more than a modern-day fairytale. The years have taught me that it makes much more sense to focus your energies where they can do the most good – not on the past, but on the present and the future.

Three things helped me drag myself out of the single-mother mire of self-pity that threatened my sanity and stability. One was my garden, which forced me to think in terms of the future (albeit one season at a time), the second was my writing, which gave me an outlet for the hurt I couldn't hold inside, and the third was my children, whose demands kept me too busy – and too distracted – to make a full-time career out of feeling sorry for myself.

I'm not sure what the biggest challenge in a man's life might be. But I do feel that for a woman, few life events can be as devastating as divorce. Words like failure and rejection and broken (as in heart and home and dreams) repeat themselves on a constant playback until the belief in a brighter future – or at least a tolerable tomorrow – vanishes.

It took years as a single mother before I allowed myself to stop envying the affection and affluence my ex and his new Mrs enjoyed. And it took even more time after that before I decided that I might be ready for a little romance of my own.

The safe, discreet and easy way to link into the interview segment of this chapter would be to end my personal divorce reminiscences here and now. And that's exactly what I did in my first draft of this book. But the honesty of the women whom I interviewed for this book quietly shamed me into telling the truth, the whole truth, even when it hurts.

Although there are many women my over-active (and unlikely) imagination envies (such as Audrey Hepburn, Anne Morrow Lindbergh and Grace Kelly), in real life I like to see myself as an untelevised Mary Tyler Moore, smiling my way through the sitcom dramas of everyday life. So it's hard for me to reconcile that sunshiny imaginary persona with the heartbreak of a divorce. Not to mention two.

A few years after my high school sweetheart said goodbye I remarried. This time all the evidence indicated – and all my friends agreed – that I'd found someone who wanted to be my partner for life. Fifteen years my senior, reeking charm, and ready for the slippers and fire routine, my second husband served as an emotional knight in shining armour for my sons and for me. For a while.

But before too long the children got on his nerves, my friends got on his nerves, and, finally, I got on his nerves. The man who had, when I was hesitant about getting engaged, sent a dozen roses to my office every week for four months and showered me with gifts from Tiffany's, began to work longer and longer hours. Within a thousand days, he forgot to send flowers, he forgot my birthday and soon he forgot his wedding vows. He was no longer available to read bedtime stories to the boys and before we knew what had happened, he had moved in with Peter Finch's ex-wife, called to tell us that he simply wasn't cut out to be a family man, and filed for divorce.

Not surprisingly, this time my self-esteem was totally shattered, and my sense of worth as a woman, a wife, even a mother was pretty non-existent. The sense of rejection – two divorces within one decade! – was enormous.

For the first few weeks after he left, I was numb with shock and disbelief, then I felt a small surge of anger (as opposed to the Mount Vesuvius of outrage I'd felt towards my first husband and his new mate), and, finally, I felt a deep-seated sense of sadness for all that we had been and might have shared. By the time his fling had ended, and his flowers and requests to come home had begun again, our California divorce had been declared final. I was still too wounded to know exactly what it was that I felt.

All I knew for sure was that I no longer loved – or trusted – him. We remain on friendly terms; he still asks, on a regular basis, if we can get remarried and I look at our time together through lenses of sadness and waste. I seriously doubt if either of us will ever be brave enough to marry again.

Shirley Conran spoke about the awfulness of divorce with more candour than most. And I was gratified that she spoke about the 'public' aspect of its pain, because the hurt of the marital goodbye is not a secretive one. The social fabric of your life – from your family to your neighbours to your friends to your colleagues – is forever altered when someone who has promised to love you till death do you part reneges on that vow.

Like most women who have seen their marriages disintegrate, I wouldn't wish divorce – multiple or otherwise – on anyone. Shirley Conran recalled:

My divorce left me absolutely devastated. I got custody of the children and he got custody of the money. It was all very painful at the time and I kicked and screamed and generally didn't behave very well at all. The humiliation was particularly painful.

I can't think of anything worse than being responsible for two children when you don't even know if you can handle basic survival for yourself. When you've emerged from a divorce you're in no condition to be dynamic and get a job and enjoy the new 'challenge' and excitement of life as a single woman.

The only thing that helps, or that helped me, was time. Eventually you accept that you can't go around blaming other people for what has happened in your life.

Audrey Slaughter describes her divorce experience much more dispassionately than Ms Conran, which may be because she chose to leave her husband; while Ms Conran had to cope with the pain of rejection, Ms Slaughter felt 'relief'.

I married at nineteen and left him when I was twenty-seven. He was fifteen years older than me and I met him virtually straight from school. If my mother had not objected to the romance and not said 'You can't see somebody like that, someone so much older' and that sort of thing, I'm sure it all would have fizzled out. But because she objected and because I was asserting myself, I married him despite her; of course she was right. I sometimes think now, watching my own children or my stepchildren making mistakes, that arranged marriages are a good idea.

When it was over the only emotion I felt was relief. I could then get on with my life myself instead of pretending that it was a lovely marriage, which it never was right from the start. The only good thing from it was two children which again came about because I was thinking that perhaps our relationship would be all right if we had a family. Of course, that is the worst reason for having children, but anyway the children turned out okay.

After the divorce I lived with another man for about twelve years, which was very happy and interesting but stormy as far as the children were concerned (he didn't have any children and he resented the boy, not the girl). So there were problems there and he was very resentful when my success was beginning to be quite strong. After him I had one year of delayed teenagedom when I did all the things I should have done then – went to parties, out with lots of people, had a lovely time, and met my present husband, Charles. We have been married seven years.

Lynda Chalker has a large, formal and impressive office and a large staff of loyal energetic helpers determined to protect the Minister from unnecessary intrusions and annoyances. In spite of all the pomp that surrounds the Home Office, I was able to sit down with her and discuss several issues, including her own painful divorce. Now happily remarried, I noticed that, unlike her other answers, her voice became quieter, softer and slower when reflecting on one of her life's most painful episodes.

Eric left in 1971 and for the best part of a year it seemed like the end of the world; we'd been married four years. Eventually I picked myself up and I re-examined the marriage and asked myself how much of its demise had been my fault.

During the last six months we were together, I threw myself into cooking classes and tried to make sure that he was *always* put first. But that didn't work. I probably really devoured work after the divorce. I changed my job the following year. And whilst I was a bit rudderless for a couple of years, within two years of Eric's going I was a Parliamentary candidate and within three years, I was a Member of Parliament.

Whilst the divorce had knocked me very hard and changed me, it also helped me. It helped me be more concerned and understanding, for example, when I worked with single-parent family problems at Health and Social Security.

Very often it's the woman who gets the rougher end when a marriage breaks up, although men whose wives leave them seem to have a very hard time of it too.

Lynda Chalker, who is now blissfully remarried, wanted to share the message that divorce may seem like the end of the world – but it isn't. It is a painful episode that can alter one's life, but needn't ruin it.

— 2 —

Criticism

Over the years I've managed to change my attitude towards criticism. I used to see criticism as a censorious threat; now I recognize it as a tool whose value is dependent on *my* use. It can be censorious or it can be constructive. It's up to me.

When I was younger – in fact, only a few short years ago – I had allowed criticism to assume the posture of a powerful enemy. It could disrupt my peace of mind, confidence and emotional security. Anything short of praise was threatening to my fragile ego. And while I still don't regard criticism as a friend, I like to think that I've managed to learn to live with the inevitable fact of life that I'm going to be subject to criticism as long as I interact with other human beings simply because you can't please all the people all the time.

I try not to seek out or invite criticism these days, but I do revel in the fact that (usually) when it does rear its ugly head I can handle it without falling apart or feeling destroyed. And the nicest part of this new relationship with my former nemesis is that I've learned how to *use* criticism rather than feel *abused* by it.

Oddly enough, learning not to be devastated by what other people say about (or to) me has also taught me to be less critical of others. At one time I could easily find fault with practically anyone. My well-trained eye would spot a ladder in a stocking while conveniently missing the stunning outfit the lady in question might be wearing. I would see the spelling error in a note from my child and miss the warm affection that practically leapt off the page. My desire for perfection (from myself and others) produced a seething cauldron of condescending criticism.

I can now ruefully admit that such a distasteful state of mind (no doubt fuelled by insecurity) must have made me a very emotionally demanding person. It's a miracle I have any friends left at all!

Perhaps being adopted as a toddler gave me the innate drive to please others – at any cost. Somewhere within my three-year-old psyche was a seed – just waiting to grow stronger – that warned me that if I didn't please others the good things (like pretty clothes, pony rides and oodles of love and attention) might be arbitrarily snatched from me. The biggest threat to the good life I had miraculously inherited, of course, was criticism.

For that reason I tried to satisfy people's wants and needs before they actually told me what they expected of me. This earned my parent's praise, the title of teacher's pet in the classroom, and the schoolyard sympathy of my classmates who knew, with the psychological X-ray of the young, that my actions were not prompted from honesty as much as from fear.

It wasn't until I entered my hormone-crazed teenage years that I had the courage to court my parents' criticism. And I was a student at UCLA before I began to earn good grades beause I wanted to, rather than because diligent studies short-circuited critical professors. And I was well into my twenties before I set the tempo and tenor of my friendships rather than admit my willingness to do anything – anything – rather than risk censure from a friend or colleague.

In spite of all that, I recall a great deal of criticism during my childhood. My parents viewed it, of course, as 'direction' or 'guidance' or 'help'; they honestly didn't think of themselves as critical parents. But my insecure youngster's mind interpreted their attempts to improve me as proof that for some unknown reason I simply wasn't – and probably never would be – good enough.

Mama and Daddy, who had gone for so long without children, had watched their peers raise families with a quiet sense of envy and reserved judgement. They felt that they knew why the neighbours, the Greys, were having trouble with their son Andy. They knew just why little Patsy Smith was bringing home heartbreaking report cards. And there was no doubt in their minds regarding what it would take to get Walter, from next door, into the college of his choice.

When they adopted me – about the time their contemporaries were waiting for their first grandchildren – my parents no longer had to limit their child-rearing observations and theories to their dinner-time conversation. With me on the scene, they could, at last, prove that their theories were right. Once and for all.

Thus began my career as a would-be supergirl. In retrospect, I don't know how I coped with the subtle but never-ending pressure, but I obviously did. I don't recall feeling manipulated or coerced in any way, but I do remember feeling that, more often than not, I disappointed my parents by not conforming to the standards – or the life – they had envisioned for me. I wasn't a Rhodes scholar, I didn't compete in the Madison Square Garden Horseshow and I never mastered Rachmaninov.

With my parents' love, encouragement and money, I managed to become a marginally – but not spectacularly – successful student. I played the piano because my mother had dreams that I might one day play the organ in church (!). I played the violin because Daddy said that 'anyone can play the piano, but the real achievement is in mastering the violin'. I was given lessons in knitting, sewing and crocheting, and riding, dancing and swimming lessons were thrown in as well. No trouble or expense was too great when it came to 'improving' me.

The result was that I tried harder and harder to be 'good enough' and I learned to be my own harshest critic. I learned, while still in pigtails, that it was easier to push myself than wait for others to do it for me – or to me.

It comes as no surprise, therefore, that accepting criticism as an adult, has been difficult. Hearing someone's opinion (and that's the operative word when it comes to fault-finding) that I had somehow erred, revived deeply buried feelings of inadequacies. And they activated something far more insidious – fear.

I know that it takes a certain measure of security or confidence to admit to fear. Because both were in short supply while I was growing up, I turned instead to impatience or anger. Inside I might be petrified, but outside I was annoyed.

The good news is that because I learned to get my fear under control I no longer 'hate' those who see my faults under a magnifying glass. And the bonus is that I don't hate myself either.

There's always room for improvement and, at last, I've learned to be grateful (and sometimes flattered) when someone else takes the time to tell me something they think about my performance, my appearance, or my achievements. I don't always agree with them, but at least now I can hear their words instead of my own insecurities.

In California, our family had a good friend who was an orchestra conductor. Although the venerable white-haired man had survived the Nazis, the tantrums of temperamental artists, and the normal rigours of an eighty-year life full of excitement and challenge, he seemed far younger than people a half century his junior. One day he showed me his secret for remaining, as he put it, 'unburdened'.

On his office wall he had an engraved plaque that read:

The only way to avoid criticism is to
Say Nothing
Do Nothing
Be Nothing

Our friend Henri was lucky because he didn't let the slings and arrows of life's self-appointed critics slow him down. Researching this book taught me that he is not alone.

Detta O'Cathain appears, at first glance, to be the archetypal, self-possessed executive. But beneath that cool, calm exterior lies a friendly, cheerful woman who is more than happy to escape the busy demands of her high-powered career for a chance to talk about everyday matters.

She doesn't let criticism rattle her, but she also admits that she doesn't ignore it either. As she told me:

I always take criticism seriously and I always look at it professionally rather than questioning my worth as a human being. Occasionally people do question your worth as a human being, but generally speaking, you find those people have a grudge to bear and they're using you to work it through. The important thing is to look at criticism objectively, as something that can be very helpful indeed.

I think I handle criticism very well because I do it on the basis of being critical myself. I always say that if you are going to be critical you have got to be constructively critical. I think one of the most appalling things is to be destructively critical, and I happen to believe in the *One Minute Manager* thing very much. I have given all my directors that book to read and I say, 'Here you're in for a one minute praising or a one minute reprimand', and I do that very well and I expect to receive it.

In fact, I very often look for criticism. I very often say to my Chairman, 'Look I'm not as good as you think I am because I think what you are doing is comparing me to your past experience or some of the people who've worked round here – they're not normal commercial people, they are people who have worked with farming organizations all their lives and not really like a real world. I haven't.' I know that some of the things I get away with here would not fit, and I know that's one of the problems I've got in my current job. I want somebody, it all sounds horribly arrogant, but I want somebody who's a lot better than I am so that I can measure up, which I strive for at the present time. I don't have anybody like that so I have to do all the pushing myself.

Shirley Conran has had plenty of criticism levelled at her over the years but she doesn't seem to have been crippled by it. She shared with me her advice for coping with people who like to point out your shortcomings.

When it comes to criticism I think the key is knowing who to (and who not to) listen to. Also, if you have a firm idea in your head of what you can do and how well you can do it, then it doesn't really matter what other people think.

Sally Burton, on the other hand, admits she can be wounded by fault-finders.

I'm very sensitive about criticism. If it is criticism about the work that you are doing then I think that is constructive. When it is actually about you as a person – how you handle yourself, that is very different, that hurts.

When I asked Prue Leith how she coped with criticism, she actually laughed out loud. Then she explained how the catering business had taught her to *use* criticism for her own means.

I hate criticism, I absolutely hate it – it is the old thing – praise flows of me like water off a duck's back and criticism goes in like knives. But I have learned that criticism from customers, and restaurant critics in general can be useful. The way to handle it is to believe them, because they don't like complaining and they don't like criticising any more than you like getting it so if you believe them, you have got a chance of fixing what's wrong and anyway it is a marvellous opportunity if somebody complains – all you need to do is grovel a bit, say you are terribly sorry and you have got it all wrong and you will try harder next time and they will love you. If a customer writes to me and says they had a disappointing meal in a restaurant, I say, 'Look I am terribly sorry, there is no point in me going into the whys and wherefores, you don't want to know what crises happened in the kitchen that night – just please come back, give us another chance, I will pay for your dinner or give you a bottle of champagne, or whatever. . . .'

He tells the whole world how wonderful we are and if he's lucky has a decent dinner when he comes back. Occasionally you get the guy who complains for no good reason, which is the same as getting the drunk in the party every so often, but in 20 years in this business, I can count on the fingers of one hand all the people who were unfair.

Jane Packer was refreshingly honest about her hatred of criticism. With a candour that only a very secure person could use she told me:

I take criticism of any kind very personally. In fact, I do rant and rave to a certain extent. Within myself I build up this defence and that is almost a barrier, arguing with myself – 'Oh I wasn't in the wrong really,' but in actual fact I take it very badly.

Jenny Agutter also admitted to not taking criticism very well. But the more we talked about it, the more I felt she was able to approach being criticized as a learning experience.

I try to take it lightly and also productively because criticism is an important part of growth. If criticism comes from an unbiased source, it's basically showing you where you go wrong whether it's in work or in life. Consequently, you can use it, because you know what it means. A lot of the time you get defensive about criticism because you think the person has misunderstood what you were trying to do.

Audrey Slaughter seemed almost ego-less in her approach to being criticized. She told me, 'I don't think I react with hurt but straight away ponder it and think "Oh right", and then I am prepared to apologize if I have been in the wrong about something.'

Pat Booth insisted that she always has time for criticism – as long as it comes from readers rather than reviewers. As she explained it:

> One side of me doesn't take any notice of it all (i.e., if I get bad reviews); but I do listen to the public. If I meet someone who has read one of my books I am intrigued to hear their opinion and will listen to every criticism they make of my book.
>
> This goes for my five novels, one photographic non-fiction book, and two photographic books. I like knowing what readers think about my work.

Celia Brayfield, like Audrey Slaughter, had a very even-handed approach to criticism. I couldn't help but wonder if Fleet Street had taught these two journalists to keep an open mind about other people's opinions.

> I guess I examine criticism, and on the whole I want to know where it's coming from. It can be harmful if it is coming from an emotional subtext. You can receive criticism that is essentially coming from someplace that has nothing to do with you. In general, I will accept sensible, professional criticism. I think I am possibly a lot more open to it than many people expect, and on the whole I am a professional, amenable person and if I can see the sense of what people are saying and it is not an issue of principle, then I am quite happy to do what they want.

Lynne Franks was the only interviewee to approach the subject from a spiritual point of view. Crediting Buddhism with helping her accept – rather than reject – other's viewpoints, she told me, while we relaxed in her office:

> I used to get very, very hurt by criticism. I still get very, very hurt, but now I equally listen to it. I always pay attention to criticism if it is justified, as opposed to spiteful, criticism. I am in a very competitive business where there is a tremendous amount of bitching from other women and I hear people whom I have never met say mean things about me – and that is very hurtful and very sad and destructive. I don't go round criticizing other people and I don't particularly dislike people who don't

like me because of a career jealousy thing, and I have a lot of that in my industry. So I find that very sad and hurtful.

When I get criticism from people I care for and respect, I listen very carefully because I know that there are areas that I can be criticized in. I know I am selfish and I know I am thoughtless and all the things that I am constantly desperately trying to change about myself. As a Buddhist I totally believe that each life that we come back, is because we are here to grow.

If I am criticized, I have made cause to create that criticism and therefore, I have to look inside and think, 'Well they are right.'

Although Elizabeth Emanuel doesn't appear to be as spiritually orientated as Lynne Franks, she too approaches criticism as a tool that can be hurtful or helpful, depending on the motivation behind it. She explained to me:

If I have done something and I am utterly responsible and somebody criticizes what I've done, then that's fair enough. I can't take criticism, however, if somebody else has got me to do something out of friendship or obligation and I'm criticized for it; then I take it very badly indeed.

If I feel I am right over something, then I simply don't take criticism very well; I get really hurt. If you do something and you know that it is wrong then that's something else. In that respect, if I know that I've done something wrong then that's fair enough. I find that when you are knocked and you are working very hard at something you really believe in, it can be a very negative force, which is one of the things David and I can't bear. It's one of the things in work that is very important now. We try to get rid of anything negative so that we can surround ourselves with positiveness. There's constructive criticism and very bad criticism. If people try to be constructive with their criticism then that's fine.

Criticism at work

Before I moved to London – in fact, one of the reasons I decided to try my luck on Fleet Street – I had a crash course in coping with on-the-job fault finding. I had a boss whose favourite pastime seemed to be telling me – and/or my colleagues – what was wrong with me and with my work.

As a chronic workaholic and hopeless type-A over-achiever, it was a rude shock to my system to inherit a boss who didn't think much of the personal or professional Marilyn. Decades of pleasing people in power had left me totally unskilled at handling someone who regarded me as his cross to bear in life.

At first I was in shock and kept thinking that my new boss and his temper tantrums were a nightmare from which I would soon awake. Then I began to get angry and decided that he was an opinionated monster who had singled me out as the escape valve for some hidden inner anger. Then I succumbed to depression and got in the practice of driving home from work with tears in my eyes. And finally I accepted that I had to cope up with this dog who was too old to learn any new tricks – and that meant that the only person who could change the situation was me. So I did. I resigned.

Since that experience, I've learned that the unhappy fate of being a boss's punching bag is one that many women share – on a temporary basis if they're lucky, on a permanent basis if they're masochists.

I'm happy to report that cruelty from an office superior frequently has the end result of an unexpected burst of achievement or accomplishment from the one-time victim. I wonder if the office bully realizes that he or she actually – circuitously – does a woman of talent a favour when he singles her out for ill treatment?

A former colleague of mine on the *Daily Mail* told me of a similar experience she had endured some years before. At the time, she was one of several women who reported to a male supervisor. My friend was young, attractive and eager to please. Her boss was an avuncular-appearing middle manager who had been passed over for promotions several times. Physically, he was an unattractive man, but his ability to handle detail was widely recognized by his superiors; he was perceived as a man who had reached the top of his own, rather small, ladder of success. He was publicly caught in what must have been a frustrating career stranglehold; his executive dreams would never be realized, but his compensatory salary provided a comfortable lifestyle for his wife and teenaged children.

Unfortunately, my friend, young, pretty and unencumbered with a dependent family, became the target for all his pent-up frustration. When it became obvious to her that she could do no right in his eyes (even though other executives admired her work) she handled the situation by cultivating mentors who could help her sidestep her nemesis boss. She eventually stopped speaking to or trying to please him. While it rarely works this way, the entire incident ultimately reflected badly on the boss, who has since been passed over for that much-desired promotion twice!

My friend labelled this sort of office bullying 'the nerd syndrome'. She noticed that young, attractive, cheerful women can become dangerous symbols to unattractive, unhappy men. Women on the way to the top can remind them of things they wanted – but didn't get – when they were younger. 'There were probably lots of girls like me when he was in school,' she told me. 'They may have been cruel to him or refused to go out with him or made him feel inadequate in some way. Once he got a little power, it was as if he could pay back all those girls by venting his spleen on me. He probably doesn't have anything against me personally, but I represent a target, a symbol of some long-ago hurt.

'But since I don't have the time or inclination to be a shrink for every hostile grown-up schoolboy, I've learned to avoid working for frustrated, unattractive males. I want to be judged on my work, not on the actions of some insensitive schoolgirl from the sixties.'

My friend's experience is extreme, but unnecessary criticism on the job can turn your working hours into a nightmare if you don't develop a strategy to make it work for you. Probably the best advice I ever received about criticism was to think of it as a tool that could either help me improve my performance or learn something about the person doing the fault finding.

Since leaving my former boss in LA – who, coincidentally, became a warm and cordial person as soon as I was no longer on his staff – I have been blessed with superiors who may see my flaws but prefer to focus on my strengths.

I no longer go home with tears in my eyes and I realize that, although I wouldn't want to repeat the experience of being bullied at work, it did propel my career into a new, more rewarding orbit.

Criticism at work used to trigger my 'fight or flight' reaction; now I let criticism propel me to where *I* want to be, rather than to a place where someone else wants me to go. I still hear the criticism, but now I know how to listen for the unspoken messages behind it.

Member of Parliament Emma Nicolson had some sensible advice for women who have to cope with office fault-finders. Relaxing in her pastel-coloured lounge, she told me:

> I'm sure that the way to deal with criticism at work, is to accept it, generally speaking, as something that is hurtful and positive, examine it and if it doesn't seem to fit the case, reject it. If it does fit, then you have to modify your behaviour. I think that if it is just somebody using criticism to try to work out a grudge against women, against society or against life, then you have to ignore it.

Novelist Pat Booth, who spends a great deal of time at her Florida home, revealed her pro-American attitude when it came to the subject of professional criticism.

> How I react to work-orientated criticism depends on who the person is. If I admire somebody I listen 100% and I take their advice. I tend to prefer writing for American rather than English publishers because I think that they are better editors; I think they are infinitely more professional.

Jenny Agutter, perhaps thinking of her new Broadway role in 'Breaking The Code', explained.

> If it's specifically criticism at work on the way you approach a role and you think that that was not what you were actually trying to do, then you protect yourself. If, on the other hand, what you were trying to do does not get the script's message across to the audience, then you have to take that criticism and apply it to your acting and make it better.

When I went to Audrey Slaughter's home – armed with my questions and my tape recorder – she told me that writers are always subject to professional criticism.

> Yesterday a piece I was doing was not right. Actually I didn't like it myself but was painted into a corner so I just said, 'I agree with you. I will do it again.' I think if it had been personal criticism rather than someone's professional judgement, it would worry me more.

Prue Leith's most critical episode came, not in the kitchen, but in front of the cameras as she was filming a daytime programme. As she remembers it:

> The worst experience I have ever had was with a television director when I was presenting a programme. I had never done TV before and I was really very daft to take it on, but by a chapter of accidents I found myself presenting a 26-part afternoon women's series with no experience. Not surprisingly I was very bad. The director was perfectly awful because I had not worked in television before and didn't know that directors were anything better than this chap.
>
> He totally terrified and made me demented because he would say things like, 'In rehearsal, you put the wooden spoon down on the right side of the olive oil bottle,' or he would complain if I didn't use exactly the same words I had used before so I thought that this was what all people in television were like and I had thirteen weeks of this (we did two programmes a week) and I was absolutely wretched and thought, 'I hate it,' so I stayed out of television for ten years – partly because nobody asked me because I was so bad the first time and also because I refused even if I was asked because I thought it was all like that.
>
> I was very weepy and stayed in this terrible hotel in Newcastle totally on my own and feeling wretched. Finally, one of the cameramen after we'd filmed about twenty of these shows, came to me and said, 'Haven't you heard of valium?' so I took some of that and then I enjoyed the next six shows. I thought everything was great and was having a great time. It was bad advice but at least the cameraman was nice to me. The whole episode taught me to be careful of what people say when they're being critical. I have since done a lot of television because I discovered it was his fault not mine – mostly.

Learning not to accept criticism at its face value is something that Celia Brayfield learned on Fleet Street and used while writing *Pearls*.

> When I was writing, my English conscience had this system of editing by committee. For the first draft of my manuscript my publishers actually had me sit down with four people simultaneously. All of them had produced long notes on the manuscript and all their criticisms were completely contradictory. In the end I simply threw the lot out of the window

because they were so silly – among the criticisms was the comment that I had got the date of Pearl Harbor wrong. (I hadn't.)

Ms Brayfield's worst work experience came with her first job in journalism.

> I was made redundant from the job but they didn't tell me that. What they said is, 'You're fired, it's not worked out.'
>
> At that time I was terribly upset because no one had said a word to me about the quality of my work. What I didn't realize was that they used to hire a trainee every three months and fire her before they were legally obliged to make her a staff member. In this way they got away with paying trainee's wages and not technically creating a job under the normal agreement. I didn't find that out until a long time afterwards when I had stayed in the business for a couple of years and I met half a dozen girls who had had my job. Then I could see what was going on. I think that is what you have to do. You have to look beyond the criticism and find out what's behind it.

Lynda Chalker knows how important diplomacy can be when crititizing others; in her position as number two in the Foreign and Commonwealth Office she has also learned to approach criticism directed at her as a tool that can strengthen her executive skills. She explained her approach to office criticism by telling me:

> First of all, I always try and examine what has caused them to make the criticism. In other words, I try to be as analytical about it as I possibly can. And if they've got a case, I think 'How would I do it better the next time, do it differently, how would I meet the reason for the criticism?'
>
> It's sometimes hardest to cope with criticism at work because you have to operate a little more in a vacuum, in other words, you have to do all the probing, perhaps rather diplomatically and personally, because otherwise if you go on repeating the criticism, the potential is there to lose face, perpetrated by yourself. It's worth doing it analytically and you should always do it – you should not brush it on one side.

Friends and lovers who want to 'improve' you

As we've seen, it's no fun coping with colleagues who choose to focus on your faults. But it's even less enjoyable to hear someone with whom you are emotionally involved tell you about your so-called shortcomings.

Those of us who are lucky, receive 'caring criticism' in small doses from friends wise enough to sugar-coat their bitter pills of honesty. Faultfinders, friends or lovers, can still be brutal when telling you what they think you need to know.

When I look back on hurtful criticism from friends, it seems their harsh words have almost always centred around my clothes. As a schoolgirl I was partially protected by school uniforms, but on the monthly 'free dress' days' I was forced to reconcile myself to the fact that my family's income and their attitude towards 'frivolities' meant that my 'free dress day' wardrobe would be alarmingly low-budget in comparison to that of my classmates. My parents didn't know, or care, about the difference that Capezio shoes or cashmere twin sets could make in a young girl's life. They were convinced that if you looked clean and tidy and had a smile on your face the world would welcome you with open arms. Much to my chagrin, I wasn't welcomed. I was 'the new girl' and there wasn't a single thing about me that made me special. My looks, my home, my parents, my grades and my clothes were ordinary. And in small schools with unfounded pretensions of the privileged classes, I stood out in the worst way.

The result of the teasings I suffered about my 'ordinary' clothes is that I grew up to become an unabashed clothes-horse as an adult. And as a mother, I made sure that my sons, whenever they weren't wearing a uniform, were dressed in the best clothes that my pay-check (or credit cards) could buy.

With the curse of a strong memory, I remember (with a cringe and a blush) the time I met a dear friend for a Saturday shopping spree. I was in my late twenties, and my friend had no knowledge of my unfashionable fiascos as a schoolgirl.

For our shopping date I had dressed in a new outfit that I felt was particularly becoming. But within seconds of greeting each other she said, 'When you get home throw that suit away. It's horrid.' I stubbornly ignored her advice, never mentioned the incident again, but her unbridled, dictatorial attitude wounded me; our friendship was damaged beyond repair.

Criticism from romantic partners has centred, if not on my wardrobe, then on my overall appearance, my taste, hairstyle, shoes, handbag, jewellery, or furniture. As with my friends' observations, however, these comments have had more effect on my attitude towards the faultfinder than on the subject being criticized. A boyfriend once so hated my handbag that he presented me with a lavishly expensive one from Neiman Marcus that he felt would be more becoming. The next time we met for lunch he made no secret of the fact that he was disappointed that I carried not the shiny new 'image-improve' bag he had chosen, but my trusty, comfortable all-purpose bag. He had wisely followed my mother's axiom. ('A gentleman should never criticize any item belonging to a lady unless he's willing to replace it') but he forgot – as men so often do – to ask the lady's opinion of the object in question.

There are two ways to successfully cope with the faultfinders. The first is to make sure that you believe in yourself – whether it be the way you look, dance, laugh, or whatever – enough to recognize an honest difference of opinion as merely that (and nothing more). The second is to acknowledge that other people are entitled to their own beliefs, which very often vary widely from our own. But by accepting their opinions as mere opinions – rather than as rules or judgements, or facts or truths to be adhered to – it is easier to handle criticism with the same distance you'd use if someone admitted that – unlike you – he or she didn't like chocolate or brandy or steak tartare.

This accepting attitude towards criticism is useful for another reason as well. If you can take away the element of struggle over the rightness or wrongness of some item you like, you can approach the conflict (i.e., the criticism) without the emotional garbage that is little more than a power play.

The more we fight against someone's opinion, the more energy we inadvertently abdicate to them. The mature attitude is to listen to their ideas, to rely on our own ability to evaluate what you've heard, and then emerge from the incident with your self-esteem and your flexibility at healthy levels.

Fortunately, I can now chuckle over past episodes of criticism from people I cared about. While I was still deeply in love with my first husband – without realizing that he was falling in love with someone else – I received a great deal of hurtful criticism from him. I naïvely thought he was giving me information that I could use to salvage our marriage. What I was really getting, however, was lots of stored up animosity and guilt-relieving critiques. He may have even thought that the more he made me cry and the more he verbally attacked me the easier it would be for me to accept his choice of replacement (it didn't).

One Sunday, after church, he told me (with a pained expression on his face) that he couldn't love me anymore because I didn't embody any of the beatitudes from The Sermon On The Mount. Desperate to hold my family together, I silently vowed to devote more of my energy to being meek, etc., but now I can view his comments with the unshakable pathos that time kindly gives to victims of self-righteous faultfinding.

We have all endured incidents where friends have meant to help – or hurt – us by sharing their opinions with us. But as the women I've interviewed know only too well, that kind of help can have its hazards.

Sally Burton told me that when Richard Burton criticized her she always felt hurt and upset because it usually focused on her appearance. 'Richard sometimes criticized the clothes I wore because he wanted me to be a bit more glamorous.'

Pat Booth declared, with a toss of her long blonde hair, 'I don't have friends who criticize.'

Fay Weldon seems to have little or no experience with fault-finders but told me that *if* a friend or lover criticized her: 'I like to think I'd listen to it to decide whether or not it's valid. I'd never expect lovers to criticize me, I'm assuming they're on my side. If they don't like anything they'd shut up because I would be the same with them.'

But most of the women I've interviewed did face criticism from people who were close to them. Not surprisingly, however, they rarely enjoyed hearing about the faults. Prue Leith, who seems to be the type of woman who could shrug off anything unpleasant, admitted that criticism at home can be hard to ignore. As she explained it: 'First of all my husband is very tactful – he has to be very tired not to be tactful and I still behave badly. I still resent it deeply however tactful he is.'

Audrey Slaughter told me that she learned to be grateful for friends' criticism after a girlfriend gave her a fashion hint.

> A friend of mine recently said, 'You shouldn't wear trousers', not because she thinks I have a big bottom but because she thinks I have a droopy bottom. She was quite right but I suddenly thought to myself 'How nasty'. But then I looked in the mirror and thought 'She's absolutely right'. I am terribly self-conscious now about wearing things that don't show my bottom. That's so trivial it doesn't wreck my life, but I suddenly thought, 'If she's been thinking that for a long time, why didn't she say something ages ago?'
>
> If my husband (Charles Wintour) finds fault I just criticize him back. The kids often mimic me. Apparently, when I tell a joke, I suck my breath in at the end to stop myself laughing at my own joke – that sort of mimicry I find not hurtful, but it gives you a strange view of yourself and you find mannerisms that you didn't know you had.
>
> I suppose I don't like it – who does like criticism? If Charles says something I will reply – just a sort of fisticuffs type thing. Professionally, if I am writing a freelance piece, I tremendously value his reaction.

Lady Porter said she would pay close attention to any criticism she received from a friend because: 'If my friends criticize me, it wouldn't be worthless. They wouldn't do it just to be bitchy.'

And Lynda Chalker said she'd rather get criticism from her friends than from those who don't have her best interest at heart.

> I'd rather have my friends trying to assist than just waiting for my enemies to pounce. I think that with friends you sit down and try again to see why and how, and there is no shame in apologizing for having got something wrong. I actually believe you have to be very honest and open about these things.

Detta O'Cathain was the only woman I interviewed who seemed to actually court criticism. In a friendly but earnest way, she told me:

> I like friends criticizing me. I'm very keen to know what people think of me not to flatter my ego, far from it, but I know that I'm so shot full of holes in terms of character defects and all the rest.

I want to know what my faults are so that I can overcome them. It's because sometimes you don't know yourself, you don't see yourself as others do and it isn't for reassurance, people think it's a great flaw in my character but it isn't just looking for reassurance. I genuinely want to know so that I can remedy it and I can change the situation.

My husband sometimes criticizes my clothes and I have to say that I don't like that. I find it very difficult and I react badly to it. I get upset, I don't necessarily show it but I do. I think at this stage, I would probably say 'tough' but before that I would probably never have worn it again in his presence. We have a very strange marriage really because I only see him from 7.30 on Friday evening until 7.15 on Monday morning. We've been married nineteen years and have a very good friendly relationship.

Celia Brayfield had a lover who seemed to enjoy putting her down. In retrospect, she told me, it was obvious that he did it out of insecurity.

First of all you have to examine how realistic it is. I had one lover who I lived with for four years who was intensely criticial because he was intensely insecure. Among the levels that he charged at me was that of emasculating him because I earned more than he did – £80 per annum more. The other great one that he came out with was, 'You file your fingernails in a low class manner.' That level of criticism is so obviously, wilfully destructive – and nothing else – that I was merely enraged. I was just very angry.

Jenny Agutter feels that people find fault when – and because – their affections are in a state of transition. In her expressive way, she explained:

It's always very hard to get criticism from people who are close to you because there's often that element – you might lose their affection. There are aspects in a relationship where if you are critical of one another it's because of a closeness and because there are things that you can probably help to change. But there's a difference when that sense of caring has gone and so they pick up on odd things. I remember someone saying to me about falling out of love, 'I remember him putting his cup down on a saucer and I remember how horrible it was' – and I thought what a terrible comment to make about falling out of love with someone. I remember someone saying to me – I hardly ever put nail polish on but once I put toenail polish on which is really unusual for me – and the person I was with said, 'Oh how disgusting, it looks totally like a whore.' What was extra-ordinary was that I didn't realize that he was breaking up with a girl who was, in fact, a centrefold. It was odd because what he was looking at were aspects of the other person's personality and putting them on me.

Lynne Franks oozes self-confidence, but even a trend setter like Lynne has her vulnerabilities. She told me that her husband's fault-finding can wound her – and anger her – like no one else's.

I suppose my strongest critic and the one that gets me most annoyed is usually my husband, because I work with him, have children with him and obviously we are closest and I find that I fairly bridle at any kind of criticism from him, but generally it is justified. I don't think anything can stop one being hurt by criticism, because none of us is perfect. I think we have just got to look at who is doing the criticizing – if it is someone we respect then we have got to look at why, if it is someone we don't respect or don't know we must protect ourselves.

Lynne is right. It makes perfect sense to hear the criticisms without being hurt by them – whether the 'information' comes from friend or foe.

The fault-finding family

Because you can't choose your family, when hostile remarks are home-grown, they have the added sting of being an inherited annoyance. It's hard to 'drop' a family member the way you might a friend or lover.

It took well into my twenties before I managed to see myself through eyes other than my mother's. A diminutive southern belle *manquée*, she had firm and fierce ideas about how a woman should look and behave. She longed for a five foot two inch, eight stone daughter with curly blonde hair, big blue eyes, and a yearning for a life of well-financed idleness. How disappointed she must have been to have her adopted brunette tomboy little girl grow into a five foot six inch, brown-eyed ambitious career woman. Often, as a teenager, she would 'tsk tsk' over my ever-growing hands and feet. She would then warn me that ladies with dainty feet and fingers were highly prized by the opposite sex. I, of course, was much more finely attuned to horseback riding or home runs than to husband appeal so my mother and I grew increasingly distant and critical of each other.

Unable to change my physique to please her, I assumed – for decades – that my looks would never please anyone. How delightful to leave home, then, and discover that there was plenty of room in this world for someone like me – someone who had spent years convinced that she was an unappealing Amazon.

Parental criticism is hurtful, but it's infinitely less annoying than hearing one's children voice their disappointment of your short-comings (imagined or otherwise). My two sons, until they entered their teens, admired me beyond any mother's reasonable expect-ations. They made no secret of the fact that they thought I was a gifted cook, horsewoman, pianist, hostess, journalist and mother. But once their hormones began to surge through their teenaged veins, their vision changed dramatically. Seemingly overnight I changed from Wonder Women into Cruella de Ville.

Being a stubborn woman, the more they criticized me, the more entrenched my 'deficiencies' became. One evening, after listening to my sons ridicule my 'Ma Walton' (in their opinion) image, my habitual overdrafts (incurred largely due to child-related expenses) and my chronic habit of walking away from potential conflicts (to prevent me from verbally ripping them to shreds), I telephoned a friend who also had teenaged children.

She soothed my wounded ego and reminded me that what I had (in my over-sensitive frame of mind) interpreted as hostility or ridicule was merely the normal process of a child establishing a separate identity. She reminded me that the more unsure of him or herself a teenager feels, the more he or she feels the need to attack the parent. And she told me that until offspring go through the motions of rejecting a parent's values, he or she cannot establish his or her own values. Out of the confusion that such looming independence inspires, comes some pretty hostile comments . . .

Her advice taught me to listen to my children's criticisms with an ear to what the comments said about them, rather than what it said about me. For example, a complaint about my reluctance to cook, meant they might be feeling more neglected than underfed.

Fortunately, when our children criticize us, our identities are usually strong enough to endure the jibes. But the faultfinding of parents, siblings and children can leave scars that take years to heal.

Celia Brayfield confided that her sister has been critical of her for years. But, with a journalistic approach to life, she views the friction as understandable even though it's undesirable.

I have constant criticism from the family, but it is clearly, nearly always, motivated by jealousy, particularly my sister. You know that song that says, 'I was born standing up and talking back' – well, she was born jealous. I hate to say this, it is not a kind thing to say about your sister, but it's been the history of our relationship; there is nothing you can do with a jealous person. Also, my father didn't like the fact that I made him wrong because I crossed his choice of profession and became part of the 'art world' he thought was useless.

Arabella Pollen told me that her family can be fairly criticial.

I get a load of criticism from my home bunch. With my husband being Italian, it is much harder for him to accept a female not being at home than it might be for an English person.

My only advice is that if you know yourself and you make an effort to judge yourself, then if somebody else criticizes you are in a much stronger position to look at it from an outside point of view. Then you can say 'Okay, they don't like that, but it may be their problem, rather than mine.' If you are happy with yourself and you have thought about it then you are in a position not to be hurt so much. I think people are hurt by criticism because they are insecure and they don't know if it's true or not. Either you have got to be able to live with yourself or you can't. I think it's one of woman's biggest problems.

And Lynda Chalker, who seems like the cosy kind of woman who would thoroughly enjoy endless family gatherings, told me that she gets the same complaint from her husband, stepmother, brother, sister-in-law and nieces.

Their criticism is that I work too long hours and they don't see enough of me but they are terribly proud of me, so what do you do? You say, 'I've only got where I've got by working such long hours.' Their criticism however, is genuinely meant with my best interest at heart and I know that.

Fay Weldon looked startled when I asked her if her family were critical and, if so, how she coped with it. In an authoritarian tone of voice, but with a smile, she told me:

Family members are in no position to criticize me, or at least I don't think so. I don't criticize them and they don't criticize me. I'm sure they get very upset, but they don't tell me about it.

Pat Booth, on the other hand, said her young son was acutely aware of her imagined flaws. But, as she explained, that was probably connected with their emotional closeness.

Pat's mother, who seemed to work all the hours that God sent, was rarely at home for after school snacks or able to cook hot meals for the family at the end of the day. Taking great pride in her ability to give her son the very 'homely' touches she missed as a child, it amuses Pat that those efforts are often met with criticism.

My son's always criticizing my food, my cooking and the way I look. But I just think that's kind of amusing and I put it down to his confusion of his love for me and his inability to properly express it.

I can't imagine Lady Porter having much patience with family squabbles, but she told me that she has not escaped her sisters' criticism.

I am the youngest child and I think older sisters always have a kind of 'sibling happening'. I think it annoys me but I try not to take any notice. I wouldn't say that they think I'm not a paragon in that department either; we have a very good relationship.

I think my advice is to get exposed more and more – the more confidence you have the less criticism hurts you. If you are a sensitive person, of course, it hurts, but you have to grow another layer and you mustn't let it get through.

Emma Nicolson, on the other hand, thinks that whatever goes on between sisters is preferable to quarrels with brothers. But in her perpetually optimistic way, she told me her sisters always seemed to have her best interest at heart.

> I have three sisters and I suspect that sisters are probably more supportive than brothers. I don't have brothers so I don't know why I say that because we are all very supportive of each other. Obviously we sometimes criticize each other because we are not perfect either on the giving or receiving end, but I wouldn't call my sisters' criticism 'criticism', I would call it helpful comments or thoughts.

Lynne Franks might appear to be so self-confident that no one's opinion could rattle her. But she told me that she pays very close attention to what her children say about her appearance. In her words:

> Well, I honestly think it comes down to self-confidence. If my kids say 'Oh, that really doesn't suit you' or 'You look fat in that one' then I will listen to them. But then I would feel free to tell them the same thing if it applied. It all depends on how it is said. If my daughter turns round to me and says 'Why on earth are you rushing around trying to pretend you are young all the time' that could hurt but I can see the day coming where she *will* say it. I still think of myself as a seventeen-year-old teenager.

Leslie Kenton, who is a refreshing mix of the ethereal and the earthy, seems to have reached a unique solution to the issue of children finding fault with their mothers. Sitting in my lounge, looking indecently healthy and young, she told me her technique for eliminating hurt feelings when family members complain.

> The way I've raised my family is completely different from the way I was raised in the sense that I'm a very demanding mother and I have always been firm – I get on very well with my children; they do exactly what I say, because I made a decision a long time ago, and I think this is an important decision to make, that I don't care whether my children love me or not.
>
> I am completely indifferent and I decided a long time ago that I was basically a nasty person rather than a nice person as far as motherhood goes, so why pretend to be anything else. They used to say, 'Mum can we go to the disco?' and I would reply, 'Yes darling, as long as you're home by ten,' and they would

reply, 'Mum, everybody gets to stay till midnight,' and I would then say, 'Darling I don't care, *you* will be home at ten o'clock' and I did that because when I was a child my parents never cared whether I was home or not and I always wanted them to care. I didn't really care about the time, *per se*, but I wanted them to know that those were the rules and that was the way it was. It's a funny thing but I think as a parent you have to really generally not care what your children think of you. If they know you're not a very nice person anyway, then you have no pretensions. But my family's been raised quite differently in the sense that, it's very important to me that things in our household happen in an ordered way. Diet is very important, a child must do exactly what's expected of him, a child is given its own privacy, its own room and so on.

I wish I'd had the strength to raise my two sons with Leslie Kenton's no-nonsense approach. Without batting an eyelash, she admits that her kids' criticisms are like water off a duck's back. I'm at the other end of the critial–sensitive scale – the one labelled 'mother-sponge'.

3

Achievement

It's a rare and lucky woman who manages to feel confident and self-assured without the scaffolding of achievement.

In my life (so far), I can plot three separate phases of achievement, each of which has differed wildly from the previous one. The first and longest phase was trying to impress others with what I had or did. This included my days as a 'teacher's pet' student, as a daughter torn between totally different parents, and a wife who was desperate for an otherwise preoccupied husband's attention and approval.

Achievement, in that mode, ranged from earning a good mark at school to eliciting laughter or pride from my parents, to wringing a compliment out of the man I was married to.

In fact, one area in which I took a great pride in my 'accomplishments' was food. These days, by way of contrast, I view cooking as something to be done only if there is no alternative. But ten or fifteen years ago I took great pride in the 'special' creations I prepared for other people.

I assiduously collected recipes and cook books and read *Gourmet Magazine* the way most women might read a novel. For birthday and Christmas nothing gave me more pleasure than a gift of some arcane entertaining paraphernalia such as special place mats, delicate olive-tongs, or a silver chafing-dish.

Countless hours of this all too brief life were spent baking home-made bread, making my own jams and jellies, and cooking entrées for dinner parties and special celebrations. I felt it was a great 'achievement' to cook foods that were special or appealing or challenging. And I now realize that each mouthful other people ate served to supplement my shaky sense of achievement.

But when I woke up one morning – alone – and realized that

decades of my life had been spent planning dinner party menus, hosting business-related get togethers, and feeding people who were no longer part of my life (because I was no longer part of *his* life), I decided that there had to be a more sensible, less ephemeral way of feeling 'accomplished'.

My next, somewhat bitter, interpretation of 'achievement' rested on the fact that it seemed more rational to devote my time to what *I* believed to be worthy of note rather than be dependent on what other people chose to think of my efforts.

This phase saw the birth of my regular newspaper columns, my two published books, my riding rosettes, and a reborn devotion to the piano, which were all designed to allow me to think of myself as a woman of achievement. I lived in a frenzied merry-go-round of doing more and more and more in order to silence the quiet nagging voice inside that wondered if I was 'good enough'.

With time, of course, I finally realized that this stage of my love affair with achievement was almost as unfulfilling as my first brush with being 'an accomplished woman'. The reason it was flawed, I now know, was because I had placed so much emphasis on 'doing' that I had totally overlooked the importance of 'being'. It took a bizarre medical incident (more about that later) to teach me that accomplishment is hollow if it's simply a matter of physical effort without a corresponding mental or emotional growth.

So I eventually grew from desperately seeking others' praise to grimly trying to earn my own. Then I reached a state of mind in which I cared less for what other people have or do than I did for what they are. It was no longer terribly important to 'get' people's admiration or even to do something I didn't think I could do (like get a perfect score on my driving test). What mattered was giving and sharing and learning how to make other people's lives better. That became the real challenge.

My father used to remind me that the one obligation each person was born with was to be an asset to life on earth. I used to think this meant we had to build or make something that wasn't already here. But I now think that he meant to teach me that our presence on earth should be 'an asset' to life, rather than a 'liability'. And trying to live with that creed – making people sense that they are worthy of your best – is a much harder goal for me to achieve than making a soufflé or playing a sonata.

Each of us, of course, has our own interpretation of what achievement is and isn't. But I was still surprised to learn that author and columnist Leslie Kenton was convinced that she was not yet a 'woman of achievement'. She too had dreams that are as yet unfulfilled, dreams that make writing health books pale in comparison.

I believe man is on this earth to become a creator with God. We have to become adult and complete individuals. You have two choices; nurture or destroy life, there's no middle, so we have to be whole so that all our faculties including the negative sides can be put in the service of life. I think and believe that the anger, and selfishness has a purpose or we wouldn't have it. We have to take responsibility and create future life on this earth because if we don't we won't exist. Unless we choose to opt for life we will destroy ourselves. I like it here and love the earth and would just love to see it go on.

To do that we have to embrace the totality of our own being – take it and direct it with intention towards what we do. I believe that's the power of intention. It really has been a matter of watching that energy gather and then I believe I'm only beginning to sense what's possible through it.

I tried to get rid of it, but it stayed with me from within and now I've made the decision to lay my head on the block and do it. I've made the decision to fail if necessary but to strive to achieve it.

Novelist Fay Weldon, whose prolific writing skills have set a standard of achievement most writers would find daunting, admits she can't foresee being complacent about what she has accomplished. Her thoughts seem to be forever focused on the future . . .

I think I'd like to get a little further on somehow, every single day. I have the feeling that *something* can be achieved every day in whatever area. I feel today is (this is a terrible way to live), but I feel that today is a rehearsal of tomorrow. In order to have tomorrow you have to work extremely hard today. The trouble is, everyday, you never get to tomorrow. You must really live *today* because you are forever planning ahead. There's always a rather unnerving sense of industry.

Lady Porter's work in the political arena demands that she rely on other people's help – or co-operation – to accomplish her goals. She told me that approaching problems this way is a relatively new skill for her, however, because her natural inclination is to follow her instinct rather than intellect.

> I can't really redefine what I want to achieve because I've now forward planned, but all this is an approach that has come to me in the last ten years or so. I used to do things very much by the seat of my pants because I'm an instinctive person. I learned that if I wanted to get someone to achieve it, it was better to plan it all out.

Sally Burton makes no secret of the fact that she considers restructuring – and surviving – her husband's death has been a major achievement for her. In a quiet voice, she told me what an eerie experience it was to be the widow of a world-famous man.

> One is aware that people watch you, they're watching – they're not coming around and helping – they're watching. So I say, 'I'll show them, I will just show them. I'll deal with this.' It is a very, very lonely experience. The awful pain is everywhere – stomach, head, everything.
>
> I now realize that I have got through it and I do congratulate myself on it and I do allow myself a little bit of congratulation that I have got through. I know I have made some mistakes but given the circumstances, I don't think I've made too many.
>
> I used to feel, before my time with Richard, that I was really struggling and really trying very hard – the way I described it when we fell in love was that suddenly all the pieces of the jigsaw came together. All the times I have tried to go off on a certain route careerwise or whatever and I have been blocked, but I couldn't understand why. When I met Richard, I realized why I had had all the experiences in my life that made me what I was and made me the person who was right for Richard at that time. It would not have worked at any other time in our lives.

Pat Booth, like Sally Burton, is conscious of the day-to-day effort involved in achieving any worthwhile goal. One of the few women who acknowledge how challenging a full life can be, she told me:

I personally think the most important thing is to be very conscious every day of what you're trying to achieve – what in that day you are trying to achieve even if it is your day off with your family. There are things to be achieved in that day and every portion of that day has got to be ticked off. I feel life is very hard, I feel it is very tough most of the time and to achieve anything for our families and ourselves you really have to work hard.

And I think if women out there know that it's tough, maybe they won't even try which might even be a good thing in its own way.

It seems to me that each of these women have made major achievements in their professional lives. But MP Emma Nicolson acknowledges that changing her lifestyle – escaping from the expectations of someone with her background – was an achievement in itself.

My working life was completely different from what I'd been raised to expect because I was brought up in a part of society where women didn't work. At the very most, you became a secretary after you were a débutante and, indeed, I did do the London season when I was seventeen while I was a student at The Royal Academy of Music. But I then went sideways and went into a proper working environment because I found that sort of life just wasn't for me. The last thing I wanted was to be a part-time secretary while looking for a husband.

While just positioning herself to *have* a career was a major achievement for Emma Nicolson, Jenny Agutter feels that learning to enhance her career was an achievement in itself. Reflecting on her professional approach to acting roles, she told me:

In terms of work, which is your bread and butter, I have to support myself and apply myself, and I'm very cold-blooded about it. I've learned to think 'If this work is going to lead somewhere – fine; but if this work makes me comfortable but it is not going to lead anywhere that is productive, let go of it.' I've learned to move on from it and do something else – even if there is a void in between – because making that break will help to move your career to the next step.

Arabella Pollen's business is six years old. But since her

marriage two years ago, she has noticed a distinct shift in her priorities. 'Achievement' has a different meaning for her today than it did five years ago. As the freight trains rumbled outside her office window she confided:

> I used to want much more than I do now. I am much more laid back about doing things. I used to say, 'I want this back by X date and I am going to get it,' and I have naturally learned that things just don't always go according to plan. So I am much more laid back and, especially since I have got a family, I probably want less in terms of success and business than I did before – my priorities have changed.

Lynda Chalker's feeling about achievement seem natural for someone whose career has been devoted to public service. In her words: 'All that matters is that it is doing something for other people; that is a very important motivator. I do think you feel a sense of achievement when you get people to listen, to understand better.'

Perhaps that sort of altruism is what achievement is all about. Few of us can – or want to – maintain a fever-pitched ambition year after year after year. It helps to recognize the problems and pitfalls that can accompany achievement, and redesign our lives accordingly.

Goals

One undeniable benefit of growing up in America is the pervasive belief youngsters acquire, as if through osmosis, that they can grow up and accomplish anything. When I was a child, I firmly believed that all doors were open to me and the only challenge was deciding exactly which one would be right for me.

With the brashness of the young, my friends and I shared a fervent belief that we were indeed 'the masters of our fate'. Whether we would become professors, politicians, movie stars or millionaires was up to us. Of course, time taught us that it wasn't quite that simple, but by the time we'd been forced to learn a few of life's hard truths, we had already acquired an inner sense of self-determinism.

That atmosphere of 'going for it' (whatever *it* might be) is one reason why America is so hostile to those who haven't been successful in their chosen field. But accepting the belief that you can set your own goals, and then achieve them, is not a trait limited by geography.

Believing in your ability to affect your own destiny would seem to be a crucial foundation for any woman's accomplishment. But knowing what you want to (and don't want to) achieve is just as important.

Although some of the women I interviewed (like Sally Burton and writer Fay Weldon) claimed that they never set goals, I found it enormously reassuring that most of the achievers I met were compulsive goal-setters. Since I can't get through a day without my list of 'wanna dos' I was relieved to know that I'm not alone.

I think that dreams and goals probably grow out of some sort of nebulous unhappiness. Surely a quest for a brighter tomorrow must have its beginnings in a sense of unrest with today; that certainly explains my lifelong love affair with goals and my never-ending dreams of becoming 'somebody'.

Although my childhood ambitions were modest ones, achieving them taught me some useful 'stubborn skills' that still help me, as an adult, pick and persevere when it comes to goals.

I used the same approach to win the schoolgirl competition for a special wrist-watch when I was eight years old as I did to get my first book written and published before the self-imposed deadline of my thirtieth birthday.

The three steps I learned from my day-dreaming father – who was better at helping me achieve my goals than he was at fulfilling his own – were very simple. But I treasure them more with each passing year.

The first and probably the most important lesson is accepting the fact that dreams – no matter how improbable they may seem – can actually come true. Once upon a time things we today take for granted (like telephones, vcrs, even a female Prime Minister) were little more than someone's 'dream'. But what makes a dream come true is the refusal to accept the possibility that a chosen goal won't be met. And that requires a certain amount of arrogance if you are an adult, stubbornness if you are a child.

The next step I learned about reaching a goal was to break it down into small bits. Books are written one word at a time, marathons completed one step at a time, etc. Many times the goal I've set have seemed overwhelming enough to paralyze me. But when faced with monumental challenges like buying my own flat, or finding a new job, I instinctively break it down into small, more manageable components (filling out the first – then the second or third or whatever – loan application, making the phone call to arrange for an interview, and so on). When you tackle your goals in smaller bits they are more manageable, less threatening, and the chances that you'll be frozen in terror at the prospect of tackling such a Matterhorn of a goal is eliminated. When enough of the small components are successfully completed, of course, the goal is eventually completed. Whenever I'm intimidated by a monumental task or goal or dream, I automatically try to handle it in tiny chunks – it's an easy way to make progress (albeit small) and build my self-confidence at the same time.

The last component I use to reach goals centres around belief. My father convinced me, back when I still believed in Santa Claus, that if I wanted something badly enough I could achieve it. Harder to accept was the realization that I'd have to be patient, work hard, and devote lots of time to reaching the goal I'd set for myself. But having faith that my goal was actually attainable was essential.

Goals help us acquire a sense of growth. Few women are so happy with themselves (or their lifestyles) that they are content to spend the rest of their days in a static environment. Some want to learn how to knit, some want to get their bedrooms redecorated, and some want to learn a new language or get a degree. It doesn't matter what goals you set for yourself, as long as you recognize that deciding what you want to accomplish – and then achieving it – will give you double rewards. The completion of the goal is the tangible prize, but the growth in self-confidence and strength is the benefit that stays with us and works to make the next goal that little bit easier to achieve.

Shirley Conran told me that she couldn't imagine life without goals. Her methodical approach is closely tied to the calendar.

I always set goals at the beginning of each year. Just as one would prepare a business balance sheet, I do a balance sheet for my private life. By no later than 7 February, when the business papers must also be organized, I see to it that I have analysed my previous year's list and formulated new goals.

Business woman Detta O'Cathain sets daily – rather than annual goals. Reflecting on my own unfinished goals, I shuddered inwardly as she explained her highly organized approach to goal-setting.

> I set goals every day. I have a diary and in my diary each day I put down what I have not achieved. Normally it's a case of 'you shouldn't have done that, you've got to do better on this', etc. In the morning I look at my business diary and see the things I've got left and say, 'Is there any chance that I can make life a little easier here' or 'I can do such and such' and that's really part of my goal-setting.
>
> At the office I have devised a sort of work sheet of items that are important, items that are urgent. I try to get out of the habit of putting the nastier ones at the bottom of the tray, but I have to say I fail sometimes.

And Pat Booth is also committed to setting goals, even though she is far more elastic about them than the disciplined Detta O'Cathain. Pat Booth described herself as someone who has been a tremendous goal-setter her entire life. In her words:

> My life is very structured and always has been. I had a bit of time off for bad behaviour mid twenties but basically I have always achieved what I set out to achieve. My big problem is I always set myself a goal and get three-quarters of the way through it then back off. I usually never achieve what I absolutely set out to achieve because either something fantastic gets in the way (like another work opportunity) or I come to the conclusion (which is my big weakness) that what I set out to achieve wasn't worth the anxiety that I am getting from it. That's a big problem for me.

Lynda Chalker's work at the Home Office makes it difficult for 'tangible' goals to be met – but that doesn't stop her from setting them.

> I don't review my goals sufficiently on a frequent basis and sometimes they, in this job, are less clear than they used to be when I was doing the Minister of Transport job. In that position, I could say, 'I want to build so many more miles of new road for the same price, therefore I want greater efficiency, therefore I am looking for sensible cost cutting,' but you can't measure foreign affairs progress like that at all.

I also set goals about personal efficiency, which can always be improved. I'm trying to adopt the management technique that you only ever handle a piece of paper once but it's a jolly difficult thing to do!

Celia Brayfield learned, while writing *Pearls*, that being over-conscientious about goals can cause problems. As she explained it:

Every year I attend a goal-setting and planning workshop and set four goals for the year. From those goals I make three monthly goals. Occasionally if life seems to be getting seriously out of hand, I will actually make myself weekly goals. At one time when I was writing *Pearls* I actually broke down the production of the manuscript into two-hourly goals. I was supposed to have written so many words by 11.00 a.m. and so many words by 1.00 p.m. and so on. It did not ease the production and I have to admit that my American editor's criticism was that it was mechanical and he was totally right. I had no trouble rewriting it after that.

Lynne Franks, like Celia Brayfield and Pat Booth, has re-evaluated her goal-setting techniques. Whereas it once centred on tangibles, it now has a non-materialistic focus.

I have always set goals. What I did before I was a Buddhist was I set these goals; I had wants – to have a house, a husband, a teacher training course, the kitchen, the successful career but they were not thought out goals – they were 'I work, I work, I work and I will work to get them.' I did not expect them to drop on me but I never looked at it as a rounded situation as, 'Yes you can have a very successful business but don't forget there is a tremendous amount of pressure in work. Yes, you can have two children, but you just don't have them. There are your responsibilities and you have to take care of them. I never realized that I *could get* everything I wanted, but that it didn't mean that I *had got* everything I wanted. Now I do have goals to meet, goals much more to do with happiness and things like peace, world peace.

Audrey Slaughter had the unique attitude of setting goals that reflected other people's growth rather than her own. As she explained her mentor-like frame of mind, I found myself wishing

I'd been able to have office colleagues with such an enthusiastic attitude.

> One of the goals I do set in a way is developing people. I like to see people at the start of their career (say – they are going to be a good journalist or whatever) and when they achieve their goal, it's like a flowering of a bloom, the nursing of a difficult plant. When they do it is as though I have succeeded myself much more than them. I have had awards and things but I always shrug at them – it's far more satisfying to see others progress.

Emma Nicolson described goals as 'the fun of life'.

And Elizabeth Emanuel made no secret of how goals had helped her. 'You have to have goals otherwise you end up running in circles. You have to know where you are aiming for and trying to get to, and to do that you have to have a good team behind you.'

For some women, setting goals is a normal part of daily life; others prefer to take what life sends. Fortunately, the flexibility of accomplishing what we want to doesn't have to follow a strict timetable. Listening to the inner 'goal keeper' can be just as effective as adhering to comprehensive lists. All you have to do is recognize which technique is best for you.

Life-enhancers

My feelings about friends have changed dramatically during the past decade or so. I used to be *so* selective that I rarely had more than one or two very close friends. Together we fooled ourselves into feeling that it was 'us' against the world. We were women who allowed each other to feel 'right' – about our looks, our opinions and our behaviour. Of course, it only took a matter of months before such an elite, mutually reinforcing relationship grew tiresome. When that happened I'd look for another 'friend' who would seek my advice and reassurance and who would 'admire' me in return. Oddly enough these so-called best friends were invariably critical of the men in my life and seemed intent on convincing me that someone better was out there, just beyond the horizon. I now see, with humbling clarity, that I had a pretty twisted sense of companionship to allow superiority – of any kind – to serve as a foundation for friendship.

Blessedly, those days are past. Although I'm not aware of inviting masses of people to share my life, I have gained a new, fluid circle of friends since I moved to England. And although we exchange advice and support and encouragement, my friends these days are not interested in competition or superiority and neither am I.

Once I lost the energy or the desire to think about what my friends could give me or how they could help me (and my ego), people automatically appeared in my life bearing emotional gifts.

It was almost as if once I stopped searching, the sought-after prize materialized. These days my friends teach me skills that make life a joyous adventure rather than a communal ego-trip.

While conducting the interviews for this book, I was struck by the diversity, decency and disarming honesty of the women I met. Time after time I'd sit, with the tape recorder between us, and think 'what a wonderful friend she would make'. The reason, I suspect, that they struck me as terrific raw material for friendship was because they each knew themselves very well. And that may be the bottom-line bonus of maturity – once you truly know yourself then you are free to give the best of yourself – as a friend or lover or parent – to others.

Lynda Chalker has strong feelings about friends.

I don't think one chooses friends. I think if you set out to do that you can get in some horrible messes. I think you find friends among people with common interests, those who have shown you immense loyalty over the years. Many of my friends go back to university days, some as far back as schooldays, thirty years. A large number of my friends date back to my time in the Young Conservatives and early days in Parliament. But I do make friends fairly easily. I also spot, quite quickly, if somebody is trying to make a friend of me for the wrong reasons, which, unfortunately, happens sometimes in public life. But I've got some very firm friends developed over the last two years since I've been in the Foreign Office. What I find in this job, particularly, is that my friends are not limited to those either living in the United Kingdom or those who are British.

They are on a much wider base, but then I've always done this. I've always been a rather outward-going person and when it comes to doing the personal Christmas card list, we find we have something like eighty Christmas cards to go worldwide long before we do the UK ones.

Along the same line, Jane Packer feels it's a mistake to try to 'make' friends. As she explains it:

I don't think you can actually choose a friend. I think friendships just happen, but every so often you will meet somebody and they're very familiar with you, almost as if you had known them for a lifetime, but I don't actually like that because I don't think you can do that. Friendships just happen –sometimes with the most unlikely people, but once they have built up, that kind of friendship means an awful lot to me. As far as choosing, not necessarily strong friends, but people that I am involved with and people that I work with, I am very selective. I know the kind of things that I like in a person and in all honesty, because within a busy working day you might have to do lots of things that you don't want to do, things you might find a bit of a chore, then to have to go out and socialize with people whom I don't particularly want to spend time with, I can't do it. I have done it once or twice and thought to myself, 'Why the hell did I put myself through that?' The next time I just say, 'I'm sorry.'

Emma Nicolson's friends come from her professional life more than her meagre personal time. Only an extrovert could cope with the numbers of people who populate her busy days, but as she told me:

The problem is the volume, the numbers of people. There just isn't space and time to see and meet with everybody who is ready and willing to share – that's my problem. I should think every week I see about a thousand people because I have the constituency, 73,000 voters; every weekend I must have seen at least 500 people because I'll be going to perhaps six different functions, perhaps two on Friday, four on Saturday and I'll be holding the surgery, which is open season for people to come and talk to you. That's only by appointment so they're only small numbers and the rest of the time is spent walking round the villages.

It's really very difficult for me to disentangle the friends and working life. Almost everybody who is my friend was a friend at some stage in my working life. I'm having lunch with my friend from the Save The Children Fund tomorrow – I was Director of the Save The Children Fund for seven years and she was my secretary for the last two, and we're very close friends. We rarely meet so she's coming over to the House of Commons – she's a great and proper and true friend but she's a working friend. I think because most of my life has been spent in work, almost everybody I know, I've come across, bumped into, worked with, shared an experience with and I think the truest friends are the ones where you've been through something together, whether it's a difficult project, working on a piece of work together, or a shared experience.

Elizabeth Emanuel feels that it helps to just accept your friends in a non-judgemental way. She told me:

Generally I don't choose friends, it just happens. You either get on with someone or you don't and I find I either get on really well or I am really cold which is a bad, bad thing and I hate myself for it. I am very lucky because I have got some very good friends, and that's really important, but I never judge them at all; we all get on with each other.

Shirley Conran prefers to focus more on *keeping* rather than *making* them. Her advice: 'I value my friends deeply, but I've learned not to go to them every five minutes for advice or reassurance. And I think my friendships are stronger because of it.'

Obviously not someone who suffers fools gladly, Lady Porter isn't aware of being selective about choosing friends. But she did confess:

I think it's a natural selection because people become my friends, people I work with and I pick people up from all over. It's a chemical thing – I'm instinctive about people, people come to me with ideas and I'm somebody who attracts people. I don't know if in the sense that they want to hitch on to the bandwagon, whatever. My grumbles would only be that I must be around people who are quick and responsible. I like to bounce ideas off others, I can't stand people who just sit there – I'm a bouncer.

Lynne Franks has a decidedly open attitude towards friendship and, unlike the other women I interviewed, spoke frankly about her platonic male friends.

Fortunately I have a lot of friends and I tend to have different kinds of friends – I have friends that my husband Paul and I have had for many years, couples who started off at the same time as we did in their own areas, generally photography or creative design who have worked very hard in order to achieve, people we have grown up with. Then I have an awful lot of Buddhist friends and they all mix over but they are all different kinds of people and I value them tremendously. Then I have a lot of friends that are more recent friends, perhaps whom I have met through work, people that I just get on with well. I have millions of acquaintances because I have so many people in my life, one of the ways I have got to look at myself is in turning off, closing off to people, but being much more open because I tend to just keep a little back. But in terms of the few people – for as with everybody, there is always just a few people that I like – I am a very open person when I do care for people. I am not a secretive person. I'm loyal to the utmost and give what I have got to give. I think I have got an ability to recognize people that are special to me and I am generally right because the people I consider very special to me – mostly men – have a lot of other people who consider them special too. I have got a lot of women friends as well, but I have found in the past three years, three or four of my closest friends are men – they are platonic friends – but if you include my husband as well it just seems I have more fun with men.

Actress Jenny Agutter told me that she has become more selective than she used to be, but it took a few hurtful episodes before she stopped being totally open to just anyone's friendship. She explains:

Early on you get very hurt by being very open to people who generally are destructive. I was brought up always trying to make things right and always trying to work things out, and because in myself there is a desire for self-improvement, and belief that things will always be okay in the end, I assume that everybody is like that. But it's an enormous surprise when you suddenly come across people who not only don't think that everything's all right but are inclined to go towards everything that is negative.

In Los Angeles you learn very quickly whether people are inclined towards anything that will help remove them from that competitive world – things like alcohol or drugs – and the thing is to have absolutely nothing to do with it. I remember one person that I had as a friend over a long period of time, I spent a long time just trying to help and there are some people that you just can't help. It was not healthy at all and it was a surprise to learn that people can actually go and self-destruct.

The difference is that there are people who are friends of mine that go through good and bad times, and that is different. I would be there at any time of day for someone that I know and love and I know that they would be there also for me. It works both ways and I think it is terribly important to recognize the things in people that are actually very similar to oneself. They become like family. There are probably half a dozen friends in the States that have become like family to me, and one has that same sort of growth with them.

Two women who admit to being hyper-selective are Prue Leith and Arabella Pollen. Both of them have husbands who consider socializing a chore, and their wives seem to agree.

Prue Leith says this posture seems contradictory because:

I am pretty gregarious and good natured and get on with almost everyone, but my husband is really very anti-social, what he likes in the way of social intercourse is a very occasional, good, intelligent dinner party for not more than six – preferably two or four – and good conversation. So the people that we tend to see are rather carefully chosen. The only exceptions are family because they are family. So I am much more selective than I would be normally, but then I have a whole host of contacts. I would not say they are really close friends, but the business and the restaurant gives me the satisfaction of lots of people. That helps me survive my husband's strictures.

But Arabella Pollen seems to enjoy the rare chances she has to be away from people. According to her:

I'm quite anti-social on the whole. I work for a great part of my life and therefore I really value the time alone with my family, and my husband is incredibly anti-social. He hates going out and he hates seeing people and much prefers to be with one person than with five. He's fiercely protective of any time spent alone, he hates going to parties, and so I have become a little that way too.

A lot of friendship is instinctive. You know that you can meet somebody new and instinctively you know whether they might become a good friend or you know whether they will be somebody you will always be nice and polite to, but you will keep them at arm's length. I do that very much by instinct. I do believe in loyalty in friends and I think that if somebody ever crossed me as a friend, I would never forgive them. I can't, and I think that once somebody does the dirty on you, they can't be trusted again.

Having said that, I am very loyal to my friends. I think that is important.

Writer Celia Brayfield has a nicely balanced attitude towards choosing people who are to share her life. She told me:

I think you make friends who contribute to your life according to where you are in it and so I think I begin with what I actually need. Like anybody I select people to whom I can relate and who are enhancing, like sunshine, like a light in your life, they are fun, good to relax with, all those things. Usually these people have nothing in common with me, they are rarely from the same background.

Leslie Kenton told me that her friends have played a crucial role in her life and that she hoped to repay their kindness:

I think friends have always made all the difference in my life. I was very ill when I was twenty-one and had this tumour and at that time the only thing to do was remove it surgically. I went to see a doctor in New York who I had seen a couple of times before and he said, 'Leslie it has got to come out,' and I said, 'I don't have any money, I can't stay in hospital very long.' And he said, 'Don't worry, we'll only keep you in a little while.' It was major abdominal surgery. He said, 'If you need a place to stay you can come and stay with my family in New Jersey.' So I said, 'No it's okay, I think I have a place to stay.'

So he put me in a hospital and I had the surgery and went home and then I said, 'Doctor, I have never received a bill from you,' and he'd say 'Oh, that secretary of mine, she always forgets to send out the bills.' And what was lovely is that he's such a beautiful man, he was not a close friend then, but years later, maybe fifteen, I saw him in New York and he was at a point in his life when he was at a real crisis. He was suffering terribly from stress and had migraine headaches every weekend and I spent three days with him and helped him to meditate and it healed all his stress. It was so lovely because I was so grateful to him for his kindness and it was so lovely in a small way to give back to him a little bit of what he gave me. But you see I believe when someone gives you something I don't think there's any reason to give something back. I think if it is given to you, you give it to others. I believe in planting seeds. I am so grateful for the kindness of others.

My next book will be dedicated to a man, another doctor who has been wonderful; I have never known that kind of love in my life. I have not been his lover, there's nothing romantic about it, but he's been like a guardian angel to me for fifteen years for no reason whatsoever. He's an extraordinarily successful doctor, a man of tremendous breadth, deeply spirited, and for some reason I will never understand – he's just looked after me. It's wonderful, because I would be lost without people and there's no way I can give back to him what he has given to me, but all I know is that if in some way I honour life and myself enough then what he's given me will be given back without me even having to try – not to him, but to others.

Claire Rayner told me that she doesn't 'select' friends. 'I don't choose, I find myself meeting people and we have perhaps some common views – we're interesting people. We're all nice, good people.'

Brenda Dean projects an aura of natural friendliness. When we met, shortly after the annual TUC conference, she told me:

I find that because I am a trade unionist I'm fortunately not restricted to the people in that group when it comes to friends. Still, I have some difficulties because I can count on one hand the people I regard as true friends. I do, however, have lots of acquaintances and find that I'm not discriminating, although I'm choosy about the individual. What I care about more is the individual – that's more important than what they represent.

Valuing yourself

I suspect that what I have learned about valuing yourself may

78

strike a chord with many readers. My odyssey began during all the years when I wasted time and effort masquerading as a self-appointed critic – of myself and others.

I managed to develop a hyper-sensitive ability to castigate myself for thighs that were too thick, a home that wasn't perpetually spotless, or my failure (no matter how slight or large) to meet any one of a zillion self-imposed goals.

This misbegotten aura of negativity extended to innocent bystanders as well. I was the first to note a blemish on someone else's face, an error in someone else's grammar, or an outfit that was not as flattering or as stylish as I thought it might be. For years I was a hopeless snob – towards myself and others. But at that stage I felt I was merely a woman of high standards and discriminating taste. I was the sort of person I wouldn't want to be friends with today.

That frame of mind, of course, made it almost impossible for me to truly value myself because my energies seemed to always be focused on what was wrong – rather than what was right – about me. Eventually, with the help of friends and books and frustration with a way of life that was proving unproductive, I became convinced that it made more sense to look for what was right than what was wrong.

Although it only took a few sentences to describe this relatively major transformation, 'becoming positive' took several years of concentrated mental effort. On an aircraft I steeled myself to find something attractive about every passenger. Every morning I reminded myself to concentrate about the wonderful things that might happen during the day, and whenever I was tempted to focus on what was annoying about a colleague or a friend or an acquaintance, I either eliminated the critical thought – or else I failed to do so and suffered guilt pangs afterwards.

This prolonged exercise in looking for good things outside myself paid the unexpected dividend of helping me discover a few nice things about Marilyn. Some lucky women, like Emma Nicolson and Lady Porter have told me that they'd never *not* valued themselves. But for someone like me, who achieved things in order to gain approval (or avoid criticism) from others, learning to value myself by recognizing the value in others became a wonderful discovery.

Although we all have different ideas of what it means to 'value yourself' I think it's a pretty simple concept. To me it's merely a matter of becoming non judgemental enough to see yourself the same way you might see your best friend. The flaws are there, but affection trains the eye to focus on the strengths rather than weaknesses.

Linda Chalker credits her husband, Clive Landa, with helping her learn to value herself.

He knows my strengths and weaknesses as well as anybody – and we share a philosophy which is whilst helping one another to recognize weaknesses, failures and mistakes, we also try to build on the positive. I do have some qualities that are slightly unusual and which when put into a team effort (which is what any ministerial office is) can result in something a bit different, more constructive. I'm a very practical person, I don't find, at the end of the day, that many long hours spent in theoretical debate does anything other than whet my appetite to achieve practical solutions for current problems.

I'm looking for practical achievement whether it be British exports overseas, whether it be working our way towards a peace plan somewhere or opening up opportunities for British business to invest, and those are goals worth valuing.

Sally Burton also credits her husband with helping her recognize her own self-worth.

A lot of learning my own value came from Richard, I think, because he valued me. I valued myself professionally, I just couldn't understand why I had the pain that I'd had or the frustration. Obviously I did value myself because I thought, 'Well, I'm okay so why isn't life going okay?' I am more at peace with myself, more at ease with myself now. I was totally at ease with myself when I was with Richard – I used to think life was absolutely joyful and wonderful. Then of course there was the horror. It was horrific for two years and then it slowly started to get better – it is getting easier and now I am quite content.

I wish that I had Richard. Life would be even better, but I don't; so with what I have got, I am quite content.

Elizabeth Emanuel learned to value herself through her work. She told me: 'I suppose my self-esteem comes from achievements, if you achieve something you've set out to get and you do it, you feel really good in yourself and if you don't then it is upsetting.'

And Detta O'Cathain also used work to bolster her feelings of self-worth.

> I've learned to value myself by achieving success in the commercial world. It's the ony criterion on which I can actually judge. It's the only way and it's come very late. Until very recently I didn't value myself that much and I can now actually say to myself that I don't think I'm worse than most people and that is honest.

Author Fay Weldon also found her value through feedback from outside herself and reflected on the role the world at large played in our view of ourselves. She told me that her sense of value came. . .

> . . . through other people's response to me. One has one's own judgement towards the world, you look at the world as if you are standing outside it, therefore you reflect back upon what you feel and it reflects back upon your own view of yourself. I think, especially young women, either by nature or by training – somehow tend to value themselves by the value of fathers or boyfriends or whatever. When young, I veered from total feelings of omnipotence to total feelings of self-application, eventually it evened out.

That sense of varying self-esteem also applied to Jane Packer. Her answer was not geared to 'how' she learned to value herself because, for her, the process continues.

> I'm still learning. It varies so much. One day I can feel really as though I am in control of my life and what I am doing, that I am achieving position in my career and then another day I just wish the ground would open up. Quite often I can meet people who will make me feel that way, will really drag me down because they are so confident and overpowering in their own personalities – they're overbearing, they believe in themselves so much that it actually depresses me to think that I don't have that strength of character or that strength of belief in myself.

Audrey Slaughter also questioned whether she had yet to acknowledge her real values. When I asked her about valuing herself she answered:

I don't know if I do yet. My husband, Charles, is always telling me that I am too distant, that I don't stand up for myself. He says, about a particular job, 'They fucked it up, why weren't you nasty? I heard you being nice. It was their fault that they did it wrong.' But I can't, I don't know why I can't, but if I lose my temper I say things I shouldn't and I find that a lack of control.

I know that I am good at my job, I know I am a fairly efficient organizer, I have lots of blind spots but I suppose I quite like myself – I am always trying to improve.

Another woman who is always trying to improve is Celia Brayfield. She admitted, when we met, that she was a 're-constructed' woman because she had changed so many aspects of her life.

I will do anything that will make me feel better about myself. I have a huge problem with self-esteem, I am basically a handbuilt personality. I envy enormously people who seem to have sprung – like that expression from classical mythology how Athene sprung from the head of Zeus – into life free of problems; they're twenty-three and do not seem to have any serious hang-ups. I was not like that. It took me a long time to recognize that valuing myself was something I needed to work on.

Lots of enviable successful women, I learned, are still wrestling with this troublesome issue. With admirable honesty, Pat Booth said:

I don't think I have learned to value myself. I'm not very introspective and I really haven't thought about myself as being valuable. I think it is important that women do work, but I don't think I'm a particularly valuable person.

Two women who have been spared the search for self value are Lady Porter and Emma Nicolson. When I asked them how they learned to value themselves they each smiled as if I'd asked them how they taught themselves to breathe.

Emma Nicholson, in her friendly, studious way, explained her feelings about self-worth by saying:

I think it is something you are born with. If it is inborn then a child has a good sense, it is then what happens whether that is fostered or diminished by the way it is treated in the immediate family probably. But none the less, even some people who are very badly treated physically or mentally, do battle through and do value themselves at the end of the day. Even though I think it's a much rougher life. I suspect that every individual is born with a proper sense of self-worth, has an enormous amount happen to it when it is young – which you can't control. You have to battle through that and we all have to help from the standpoint that everybody, each individual, is as valuable a human being as the next one.

Lady Porter – who seems to have enough bottled-up energy to answer all of Westminster's power needs – told me:

I would say I've never really undervalued myself. At school I was always a 'born leader', whatever that means. I was extremely naughty, hated every minute, and was very anti-establishment – exactly the opposite to the way I am now actually. There are still some seeds of that around. First of all I think it must be based on achievement, doing something on your own, not as somebody's mother or daughter.

Lynne Franks, whose refreshing honesty offers additional insight into the way she copes with life's challenges, has discovered that loving yourself can be one of life's most difficult assignments. Here are her thoughts on self-worth:

I am still learning to value myself. It is one of the hardest things in the world to learn to value yourself, to learn self-esteem and to learn to love yourself. A book I recently read said the problem with us human beings is that we are always looking outside ourselves for happiness and we think that if we have the perfect relationship, that is going to make happiness. But we can never expect to find the perfect relationship outside ourselves, so until we learn this self-esteem, until we learn this love of ourselves, until we respect ourselves, then we can't expect other people to find it. It is difficult, but I do love myself.

On the other hand, I have to be careful of over-confidence. Ego can be as damaging as lack of self-confidence. I do love myself but I have to watch over-confidence. It is a thin line, but accepting it and being aware of it can help ensure one doesn't get sucked in by it. I have to be surrounded by people who have their feet on the ground and will tell me to shut up.

Also aware of the power of love, Arabella Pollen credits her parents' attitudes with helping her to grow into an adult capable of acknowledging her self-worth.

> If you don't value yourself, other people are not going to value you either. I really do believe that people make their lives what they are and in order to do that you have to believe in yourself, value yourself, and criticize yourself. But at the end of the day you have to say 'Well, that's what I am and if people don't like it. . . .'
>
> I think my parents have got a similar sort of attitude in lots of ways and I think that my feelings came from them. They have always taught us to really value ourselves. And they have always given us a very secure upbringing. Although they had been divorced, they always kept us very close.

Brenda Dean became a household name in 1986 during the Wapping dispute between SOGAT and Rupert Murdoch. But becoming the first woman to head a labour union hasn't affected the way she views her own value.

> I certainly don't value myself through what people say I have achieved in my life; I don't take any vain pride in that. I don't feel, as some of my colleagues do, that this is my whole life. I really feel I could be just as happy in something else. I think I have learned this about myself through a number of crises I have survived. Last year at Wapping was one where I didn't know if I would survive either in my job or physically.
>
> One thing I do value highly is my honesty. It might sound like an ego boost, but a colleague of mine said to me that he was talking to someone who asked 'How does she get that honesty?' I value my honesty and sincerity very much; last year it would have been easy to lose it.
>
> What you've got to remember is that I come from a very ordinary background. I had no university education. I never had any great expectations in life. I had no yardstick. I never regarded myself as something special. I never came top of the class. *So* with everything I achieved, I suppose there was a bit of wonderment. Every test I have been through started on the blank sheet that I started with. I don't have any university colleagues who have done well in their careers for me to compare myself with. I didn't know myself that I *did* value myself to be

able to do these things. Last year, for example, I realized that I had stamina that I hadn't known I had. Of course, I have got lots of negative sides too and can be irritable. But I try to approach things from a common-sense point of view; I am not saying it is because I am from Lancashire, it may be my social background, it may just be a part of the world I came from, I don't know. I do know you were never allowed to get above yourself, you were always put down, so I've probably inherited a common-sense approach to my own value.

Feeling good about ourselves is vital because lack of self-esteem can cripple any woman's efforts to meet her goals. Without the calm inner assurance of being comfortable with yourself, it's practically impossible to find the confidence and care needed to experience a full life.

No matter how long it takes, the search for self-esteem is every woman's worthy quest.

Tenacity and perseverance

I have chosen two words to describe this section but they are little more than synonyms for the unpalatable word stubbornness. I've frequently been chided for being obstinate but I know inside that it's a trait that has helped me achieve 90 per cent of what I've ever accomplished.

Of course, it takes a somewhat inflated ego to refuse to be budged when facts, authority figures or logic suggest that you alter your course of action. But part of resisting what others advise must stem from feeling that you know – better than anyone else – what is right for you.

I've had two cases in which I could tangibly feel myself digging in my heels and resisting the 'voices of common sense'. Refusal to accept what I'd been told by others changed my life, and, I have no doubt, enhanced not only my self-esteem and confidence, but my lifestyle as well.

The first incident took place in the late 1970s, when I was going through my first divorce. My husband had stopped by on a Saturday morning to pick up the boys for his regular visitation. At this stage in our separation I was still anxious to please him (in case he changed his mind) and I'd made some coffee for us to drink while we waited for the boys to collect their playthings.

I have been a keen needlepoint addict for years, and at that time I had chosen a rather intricate bargello design that I planned to use as a seat cover for an old bench. As we made our stiff small-talk I showed my husband the project and explained how I'd chosen colours to match the drapes in the living room, where I planned to use the re-upholstered bench.

With quiet solemnity he shook his head and said to me 'Don't you understand, Marilyn. You're simply not going to be able to hold on to this house. It's too big for you, the upkeep will keep you in debt, and you would be wiser to move into a two-bedroomed apartment.'

My husband, who is now chairman of the board of a bank and a millionaire several times over, was right. The house soon became a burden, the upkeep stretched my budget to the breaking point, and I would have been wise to listen to his erudite financial advice. But emotionally I knew that losing the house would represent more than the sale of bricks and mortar. To me that house was the stable childhood I'd never had; it was my children's home; it was the only security my then-traumatized life knew. To say goodbye to that green-shuttered house would have been akin to saying goodbye to an important, irreplacable part of my peace of mind. So I persevered, I ignored the advice of someone who had forgotten more about finance than I would ever learn, and I managed to hold on to our home. I sometimes had to take on extra work – holding down a job during the day, finishing writing assignments at night when the boys were in bed asleep, and then taking on typing jobs at the weekends – but the house remained in my name. It does so still today. But had I not been so stubborn I surely would have listened to what someone else thought was best for me or abandoned the dream when the effort seemed more trouble than it was worth.

The next time tenacity and perseverance helped me was when I decided, against all odds, to live in London. During the summer of 1985 I went to twenty interviews, hoping to learn what opportunities might be available to an Anglophilic American journalist. A string of sombre men told me that although my portfolio was impressive, I would never be able to find work on Fleet Street.

My 'disadvantages' were recited to me in a mournful and dismissive litany. I was a woman, I was a foreigner, I didn't have a firm sponsoring my move over here, I wasn't a member of the NUJ (National Union of Journalists), blah, blah, blah. I still don't know how I managed to keep from being terminally depressed over these pronouncements, but from somewhere deep inside a little voice kept reminding me that sooner or later I'd get what I came after. It took an additional two months of scrambling once I returned to Los Angeles, but eventually I spoke with Sir David English of the *Daily Mail* and learned that they had an opening. If I wanted to hazard my chances as a freelancer they could use me on their staff. Once again I learned that well-meaning advice is not as reliable as the little voice within that prompts you to follow what the inner you, rather than someone else, knows to be the right path.

It's true that I might have more money in the bank had I sold my green-shuttered home and I might have a smoother-running life had I stayed in Los Angeles. But I feel that opting for what I knew was the right choice gave me dividends far beyond what I could have earned by taking the safe route.

Pat Booth's 'little voice' propelled her right out of London's East End into a world she knew was right for her.

When I started out, my main goal was to get out of that East End environment that I lived in; my tenacity came into play when I was determined to become a model against all odds. I was far too short, far too fat, I wasn't the right 'look' at all and I had a Cockney accent. Those were the sort of things in England, with the class thing going on in the sixties, that you had to fight enormously hard to get through. Eventually, luckily, the Beatles came along so it changed things, but prior to that it was very difficult to succeed if you were from a working-class background. So that's where my tenacity first came into play.

I then became a top model in England and Paris. Everything I have ever done, people have always suggested that I couldn't really do – every time I change careers my tenacity always comes back into play and that is the thing that pushes me forward. I changed careers from being a model, and at nineteen I had shops, boutiques in the Kings Road. I had five shops in the end, no idea how to run a shop. But at the time I thought that was the thing to have and I wanted to invest money. Luckily that's how I made quite a bit of money initially. I sold those when I was twenty-eight, and became a very successful photographic journalist and photographer. Then, around five years later I decided to become a writer, so I changed careers many times and that takes both tenacity and perseverance.

Elizabeth Emanuel and her husband learned about 'stick-in-it-iveness' when they decided to open their own shop. As she states:

We had a real job trying to convince people that it was a good idea and we had to battle against everybody including my parents and our accountant. But if you really believe in something you have just got to go for it and if people are negative, you change to somebody who's on your wavelength and can share your vision. It's an important thing to succeed and surround yourself with people who want to go for it. Now the shop has taken off, and it's a great feeling to prove everybody wrong. It took us about three years to get it together because we were reliant on the financial requirements of getting a shop together and we had to persuade other people that it was the right thing to do. But there was no giving up.

Fay Weldon has very strong feelings about tenacity and perseverance; I, for one, would certainly never underestimate her ability to follow through with her stated goals. She told me:

I am tenacious and persevering. But then, whether this is choice or necessity, I don't know. What on earth does it mean when people say women are strong? You keep going or else you starve and die. People have to be tenacious and persevering to cope with events. And I was, by necessity, tenacious and persevering – it doesn't seem any different to what anybody else does when faced with various circumstances. When told I couldn't do something, I taught myself to. I never listen to that kind of talk. I was not given to believe in other people; it was only when I became a writer that anybody said, 'You can't do this', but I did it anyway. Again, if anyone does say, 'You can't do this' or if they reject something, I then become instantly defiant and make sure somebody does feel sorry afterwards or 'I will show them'.

Prue Leith, whose exploits in the catering business were retold with *abundant* good humour, admitted that tenacity was a crucial ingredient of her success.

I am sure doggedness is the most important quality and luck

Jenny Agutter

Celia Brayfield

Pat Booth

Sally Burton

Lynda Chalker

Shirley Conran

Brenda Dean

Elizabeth Emanuel

Leslie Kenton

Lynne Franks

Prue Leith

Detta O'Cathain

Emma Nicolson

Jane Packer

Arabella Pollen

Lady Porter

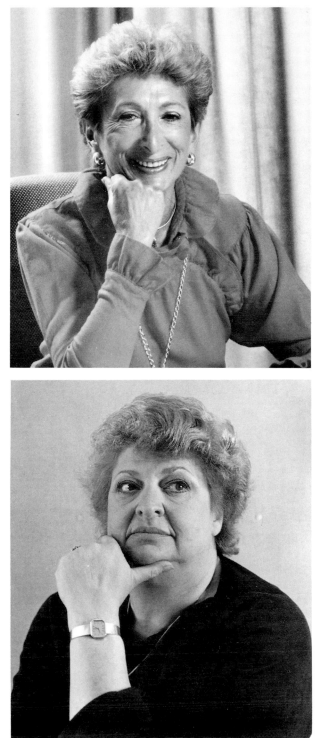

Claire Rayner

Audrey Slaughter

Ruby Wax

Fay Weldon

helps. I can't give you a specific instance but there have been times with every contract or job or restaurant or anything I have anything to do with when it has been tempting to quit. For example, with the catering company – fourteen or sixteen years ago – I just seemed to be in a muddle. I was trying to run the restaurant and the catering company in the city and I had these geographically split businesses. For the first time I had my companies in different places. The company's managing director at the time had a nervous breakdown, and the business went to pieces. I was getting complaints from customers, contracts were lost, and the only thing that stopped me selling or giving it away was that I was going to make people say Leith's was a terrific company.

Lynda Chalker accepts that being a woman in politics means she must try that extra bit harder.

I'm a very typical Taurean, which means I'm very tenacious when I want to achieve something. In a sense, that happens all the time in my constituency; problems that are brought to a Member of Parliament are frequently those which the other level of local government or regional central government haven't been able to solve. You have to have tenacity in order to get somebody that pension or somebody their rightful entitlement in housing or whatever it may be. I've used it in government too. When I've been determined that we needed to change the way in which we did something. It is even more essential for a woman because the men, if it doesn't suit their purpose, can use all sorts of tricks; it's born into them, I suspect.

Former Editor of *Working Woman* magazine, Audrey Slaughter, told me that her greatest strengths were her tenacity and perseverance. She explained:

I have gone on despite advice, despite everything, doing what I thought is right. When I first was an editor, by accident, back in the 1960s, it was a magazine already on the skids, about to go under, somebody else had started it, it had had twelve issues, and each one had gone lower and lower and lower. I started to change its tone of voice and other things. Teenagers were a new phenomenon then, in 1961, and therefore many established issues didn't work because the kids didn't understand. I really had to fight all the way through to bring out a booklet called 'Contraception and the Single Girl'. There was a great row but I stuck to my guns and won through. Then with *Working Woman*, which took me ages – we had to go through sixteen to eighteen people first to raise the money.

Emma Nicolson is no stranger to tenacity, and I marvelled at her fighting spirit when she told me of her struggles.

It was tough for me being a student at the Royal Academy of Music because I was born with a significant hearing handicap, so I had to work very hard to fulfil as much musical potential as I had to. I did piano, singing and cello at the Academy and it was difficult.

And certainly, when I went into computers, having given up maths at the age of eight, I had to battle and battle and battle to understand a fraction of what was going on. And to become reasonably competent at my field of computers was a terrific battle, but nothing is worth it unless you have to fight for it. You don't value things, it's not as much fun. I think the fun of setting yourself high goals is that you then have to fight extremely hard with yourself to achieve them. You've got to pull out all the stops, you've got to use all your talent and more that you haven't got. I've definitely had to fight a great deal all the way down the line to achieve as much as was possible of the goals that I've set myself.

Arabella Pollen told me that there was more hard work than glamour in the 'glamorous' fashion world. Without perseverance, she told me, she wouldn't have achieved much in her field.

I have been tenacious by sidestepping all the times when I have thought 'I have to get out because it's just too hard, too awful.' You have to just say, 'Forget it, I will do it, I will succeed and I don't care what anybody says.' Of course, in my business you get so much mud thrown at you and if you don't just gloss over it you get bogged down in it and so I think you just have to go on despite what people think and you have to win people's respect.

I was faced with a lot of problems because I have made a lot of mistakes and it would have been really quite easy to crawl under a stone, but I think once you have done that then you can't save anything else. I think you just have to say, 'Okay, so I have made the mistakes, I've been a complete fool, so what, everybody makes mistakes.' You have just got to approach life like that.

Lady Porter told me:

When I look at people who have succeeded I find they're not always the most able people, they're the ones who have hung on, persevered, and also the ones who've been prepared to be there. Just to be there can help you get there. So I would say it figures very high indeed, never ever give up, just keep going.

In council work you have got to do that all the time. You start with a basic idea – I joined the council because I wanted to clean up the city because it looked dirty back in 1974. The first time I went to the Director of Planning I said, 'Look we've got to have a new way.' And I said, 'Never come to me with negative thoughts, you'll get nothing out of me.' I say that to him now. 'If you say you can't do something I will chop your fingers off. There's always a way, you must look at it differently.' I've been saying this and going on and on about a cleaner city campaign. When I said I wanted sponsored litter bins, my own city planners said, 'You can't do it, you'd have to have planning permission for every bin.' Well, I've got 600 or so out there now, and every other council has got them too. So I usually just go on and on, banging and nagging and nagging.

Lynne Franks, calling her horoscope into play, told me of her specialized brand of tenacity.

I don't have discipline as such but I have tenacity. I have a low threshold of boredom and I shift on to new things – I am an Aries – a terribly typical Aries, so I like shifting around all the time. If I feel that a situation – it depends on the circumstances – if this situation is not right I will just shift off and move on. I have tenacity and perseverance in wanting to have a good life and I am not going to suddenly give up anything if I am involved, but I am also not going to hang on just for the sake of it.

.But my favourite approach to the art of learning the value of tenacity was related by Celia Brayfield. She used a DIY project to change her feelings about herself and her ability to never say die.

I never thought of myself as tenacious and I always thought that I had no stability, I just kept flitting from one thing to another.

The experience that changed me was making a patchwork quilt. Towards the end of the 1960s my boyfriend had a very large number of psychedelic velvet trousers, which he had worn through in various places because the workmanship in these was also pretty psychedelic. So I decided to make a patchwork quilt out of them and it took me three years. At the end of the project, I looked at the quilt and thought, 'I have perseverance – nobody's going to tell me I don't.' And I put it on the bed and looked at it every day for several years and after a while, I had internalized that idea. I was about thirty-two and from then on I could look back and see that I *had* been extremely persevering.

Brenda Dean told me that she is acutely aware of her ability to persevere when the going gets tough – and it has been her colleagues who have brought this trait to her attention!

When I try to do something and have not been able to achieve it, have pushed forward, and still not been able to do it, I have taken a step back and tried to analyse why. I have not said 'that's it, now I'll leave it'. I think if it is something I really believed in I wouldn't just let it go. About work, I would go and talk to colleagues and then try to approach it from another way – a pragmatic approach. So I can be single minded, but try to be a bit pragmatic about how I actually achieve that.

I do realize that sometimes I assume that everybody is on the same wavelength as me and they're not. My colleagues say working with me is like being on the motorway at 100 m.p.h. without a seatbelt on.

Tenacity is something I do admire in people who have it. I think if you're not careful it can border on nagging, but I think tenacity and perseverance must be part of any successful person.

So whether you have to be bloody minded, a nagger, stubborn, or just plain inflexible, remember that tenacity and perseverance have played a role – to varying degrees – in the lives of the women who comprise this book. Soon they may play a part in your next success . . .

4

Frame of mind

Many years ago, when Irish nuns were trying to educate my American brain, a teacher interrupted one of my rambling descriptions with her favourite quote from the Talmud: 'We see things not as they are, but as we are.'

Her gentle reminder has survived the years to remind me now, decades later, that even if I can't always control what happens to me, I ought to have some control over how I react to these events.

I wish I'd learned some of these lessons at an earlier age, but evidently fate had other plans. Where, I sometimes ask myself, would I be if I knew at twenty what I didn't learn – kicking and screaming and fighting every inch of the way – until my mid-thirties? How I envy my friends who were lucky enough (and wise enough) to spare themselves (and their loved ones), the painful lessons I have endured.

If there were an overall frame of mind that can help make life less of a struggle and more of a celebration, it would be the assumption that good things are coming your way. It seems to me that most of the events I now regret stem from actions precipitated by fear of imagined catastrophes or feelings of victimization by people I perceived to have power over my life – in other words, victim fantasies.

How much happier I would have been if I could have replaced those fears with a quiet sense of inevitable good fortune. Unfortunately, I all too often allowed my ego to interfere. My feeling was that I could be the master of my fate only by clenching my teeth, girding my loins, and forcing events to go the way I thought they should.

This, of course, took a great deal of energy and demanded that instead of remaining open and receptive to others, I focused all my attention on what I *thought* was in my best interest.

What frequently happened, alas, was that my home-grown paranoia and self-centredness sabotaged my efforts.

Now that I have come to accept that there are unexpected benefits from even the most unwelcome events, I've managed to subdue my former companion called fear. Life is decidedly easier when you ask yourself 'What lesson will I learn from this chapter of my life?', instead of 'What will go wrong next?' 'How will I manage?' or 'What if I fail?'

One of the best bonuses, for me, has been the additional friendships that have come my way since I stopped waiting for life's catastrophes to pay their respects.

The women whom I interviewed for this book were more than willing to share their thoughts about various aspects of life-enhancing attitudes.

Emma Nicolson, who struck me as one of the most serene women I'd met during my research for this book, reflected on how being a single woman had influenced her frame of mind. As a first-time bride in her forties, she felt that independence had shaped her attitudes as well as her lifestyle.

> Sometimes I look at my friends who got married when they were eighteen to twenty and I see how so many of their talents have been stifled by that lifestyle and I think it is very, very sad. I think that all the way through life whether it is best friendships at school, whether it's feeling strongly about somebody of the opposite sex, whether it's family relationships, whether it's friendships (and many, many friendships, I think, can be much stronger than many marriages), that half the rough and tumble of life is learning that if somebody sees you differently than you see yourself (whether it's a child of six when you're at kindergarten or whether it's something much later on with somebody of the opposite sex or even the same sex) the important thing is to recognize that it is not necessarily you. It may be them and their misjudgement, their lack of under-standing, their lack of vision. It's important for people to realize that it probably has little to do with them as themselves.
>
> On the other hand, it's also important to remember that you learn from every relationship whether it's a success, a failure, a trivial or a profound relationship. You also learn a lot about

yourself. So I think each time we reach out to another person, on whatever level, however small, we have the power to make it both a learning and a giving experience.

Speaking on a less abstract or objective level, journalist Audrey Slaughter told me that much of what others might see as apparent stoicism was a frame of mind inherited from her parents. They both suffered several set-backs, including business reversals, job losses, and the deaths of two sons while Ms Slaughter was growing up. She told me:

When times were bad my parents never went under or wrung their hands, they just got on with their lives. So I learned you just don't winge about life's problems. All these people who moan about their bad luck or whatever annoy me. I don't think there is anything like good luck or bad luck. A bit of good luck is possible if you inherit money or win the pools I suppose, but to a large extent I think you make your luck.

Jenny Agutter is almost two decades younger than Audrey Slaughter, but she is old enough to realize that a bit of introspection can pay dividends. As she words it:

The thing is recognizing your strengths and weaknesses. As you grow up you recognize what your faults are and then you deal with them. You can't necessarily change yourself entirely but what you can do is recognize where you can go wrong, and then just move on; it helps to recognize early.

Prue Leith credits her ability to take risks to a simple process of comparison. By believing that you can do what other people have done, untapped resources of skill, bravery and confidence can magically be yours. Ms Leith told me that even her son shared this belief in the 'double' and she shared this anecdote to explain.

I think that it's helpful to tell yourself that other people have been here and survived this situation. My little boy went on one of those Outward Bound mountain-climbing-type holidays. When he came back I asked, 'Was it frightening?' and he said, 'Yes, I was absolutely terrified. When you were on the mountain and knew you had to let go, it was terrifying.' So I said, 'What made you do it?' and he replied, 'I kept saying, other children have done this before. If they had been killed my mummy wouldn't have sent me.'

But he got his courage by saying, 'I'm not the first person absailing down this mountain, other people have done it, so it's got to be all right.' There's nothing – you might be the first woman on a major Board or anything challenging but there's nothing that nobody's done before – if you remember that you're as good as them, you'll do it.

Sally Burton, unlike so many women today, is not pursuing new challenges. With the knowledge that bereavement is a transitional state, she has chosen to be cautious rather than competitive.

I'm not chasing anything because I am aware; I know it is three years since Richard died – but I'm still floating, I'm still trying to find out what the future holds. My eyes are wide open and opportunities are coming my way, but I still realize it's not the time to fight and run after anything, because it could be the wrong thing. I must just stand back and see what comes my way and the logical thing will have the correct avenue – it will open up and I will see it.

Public Relations maven Lynne Franks sums up her contemporaries' frame of mind by reflecting on the worthwhile benefits of caring. Her volunteer work and her political activism are two ways in which she feeds this need. But, as she puts it, everyone can care in their own way.

This is the generation of the caring age, the real caring age, as opposed to the 1960s where people cared, but because they were so into tripping out on acid, they never really had the time to do much about it.

'Tune in, turn on and drop out' was what it was then; now it is 'We want to give, we want to earn, we want to live well, we want the best for our family and we want to give as well.'

This movement is only just starting because people aged about thirty-eight to forty-eight are now at the peak of their careers. And they really are today's caring people.

Health guru Leslie Kenton credits motherhood with changing the way she looks at the world. Curled up on my sofa she explained:

When I was eighteen and I had my first child, it changed my whole life in that I realized that love exists. It's real and it is not merely something that poets write about in books; you can touch it, it's the most powerful thing in the world, and if love exists then you can build a whole system on that. That's what I've tried to do.

Atmospherically it's a long way from my flat to the Home Office, but in Lynda Chalker's office I heard an equally heartfelt opinion about 'attitude'. Rumaging through her impressive mahogany desk, Ms Chalker tried to find the 'talisman' that guides both her personal and professional lives.

I've still got a letter somewhere that my mother wrote to me when I was first at school in the 1950s and in it she uses that wonderful quotation from *Hamlet* 'This above all: to thine own self be true . . .' 'Be true to yourself.' She told me 'never do anything that you don't actually believe in,' and it's been very firm, good advice.

Claire Rayner, who advises untold numbers of women how to solve their problems, learned, as a youngster, the foundation for approaching her own difficulties.

A whole lot of adult life is governed by childhood experiences. If you're fortunate enough, and I think I was, you get pitchforked into a situation where you have got to start thinking for yourself and you learn. I can honestly say from the age of fourteen or fifteen I was emotionally free. When you've got that it's great and I had ten years of total emotional freedom. I cared in a general way. I had no guilts. All I had was a deep intention to do what I wanted.

Detta O'Cathain learned about her real motivation to achieve only last year, when her father suddenly died.

My father died suddenly, we were extremely shocked. He went on holiday to Turkey last Christmas and he was in marvellous form and I saw him off at Heathrow. The following Monday, the 29th, I was at home with my cleaning lady and I said to her, 'I got some book tokens for Christmas, let's go to the book shop.' A lady came to the door and said, 'I've got some frightful news for you, your father's been found dead in his hotel room in Turkey.' My world just fell apart.

He had moved from Ireland at seventy-five to live round the

corner from me for the past two and a half years and I admired that man. I just really fell apart, but not initially. I went through all the problems because I had to manage everything. But it was towards the end of February that it hit me that there was no purpose in life because my husband really would be quite happy if I didn't achieve, he would be happy for me to be at home. I can understand that, but my father was so proud of things that I did, and I did things because we were such a family of achievers and I wanted to show that I could achieve something as well. I'd been doing that for thirty years and suddenly there was no purpose.

Leslie Kenton's frame of mind is more spiritual – yet less religious – than most people's. She told me that intuition and stubbornness were responsible for her progress, both personally and professionally. In her words:

I think that being stubborn is probably the most important thing in the world in my life. The great power in human beings is in intention, if the intention is strong enough, you can do whatever you have to do but you have to keep with it.

The book I am writing now is one I have been researching for five years, I was very frightened of it. I don't know how to write fiction, I have never had any confidence that I could do anything and yet the idea possessed me, hung on to me and pursued me and I couldn't get rid of it. I know that if it is going to succeed, how it is going to succeed is not through skills or knowing what I'm doing. The need and the intention to do it is so intense that it makes you follow that intention and that need was created in me by art.

The most succinct (and strong) statement about a beneficial frame of mind came from the novelist Pat Booth. She advises all women to trust their inner instincts and accomplish whatever it is they want out of life.

Sitting in her St John's Wood home, she returned again and again to the message she felt every woman should receive.

Don't listen to what anybody else says and don't get waylaid or swayed by other people's feelings. You have to be very determined about what it is you are trying to achieve. It might be to be the best mum in the world – you listen to that. Don't listen to anyone else – listen to your own moral imperatives. Listen to what it is you are trying to achieve and then do it.

I couldn't agree more.

Know rather than be known

Once again, we've reached a topic that makes my face go red because there's a bundle of memories cataloguing the times I behaved in a way that worked against me instead of for me. My parents moved house so often during my childhood that the bulk of my school years was spent being the 'new girl'; my life skills in this department left something to be desired.

Being endlessly relocated set up two troublesome emotions. First, it prompted me to imagine the perfection of families who had solid, unmoving bases. This in turn led me to envy kids with home-based stability in their background; I gave them an un-earned, imaginary power over me. Secondly, being the new girl made me anxious – over-anxious – to be accepted by my peers. I knew I wasn't one of them (after all, I was, hated word, 'new'), but I wanted them to want me to be one of them.

Painful as it is to recall, this led me to maniacally desire their approval. I was desperately seeking acceptance; as is often the case with this sort of personality Catch-22, I became my own worst enemy. Hoping against hope that the all-powerful *they* wouldn't reject me, I went out of my way to try to impress total strangers with my 'worthiness'. With time and a few rejections, of course, this quest led to trying to convince others of my 'superiority.' And eventually, I looked around and discovered that I'd driven away the very people I had hoped would be my friends.

Not until I had spent several years in one place (which meant my mid-twenties) did I learn that a newcomer's role is to know rather than be known. Just as the body's bloodstream is defensive towards invaders – even health promoting ones – humans are naturally wary of the new kid on the block. It takes time, and non-threatening behaviour, to prove to others that, (a) you don't mean them any harm, (b) you want to be friends for the sake of companionship, not because you want something from them, and (c) their lives will be better if they welcome you into their circle.

Moving from Los Angeles to London was the first time in my life I could remember wanting to learn about other people more than I wanted to tell them about me. Using my ears more than my mouth made the transition much easier than it had ever been during my umpteen other moves, even ones that were only from one Californian town to another (rather than from one continent to another).

For me, the hidden problem, again, was fear. Because I was afraid that people might not accept me, I tried too hard to 'win' their friendship. Had I been able to relax and accept that, given time and encouragement, I could have as many friends as I wanted, I might have been able to eliminate the frantic search for approval that, in the end, left me feeling angry, confused and, ultimately, lonely.

When I spoke to Pat Booth about the challenge of being in a different environment, she had plenty to say about being the 'new kid on the block'.

In America I still feel very much the outsider; I'm not comfortable. My roots and my thinking are very English, very entrenched in the class system, I'm very aware of all that. America is very refreshing because it doesn't have that, but at the same time my soul cannot really take root.

I have been going and coming all my life – I used to model in America but because my parents were still alive I wouldn't leave England, but when my mother died a few years ago I moved more or less fully to America. I moved there about three years ago. I was never really comfortable there; I'd only spend a maximum of three to four weeks and then I always ran home.

At first I felt very threatened but I learned that you can be whatever you want in America. I don't think you can go into other people's society and try to live as you lived in your own. You have got to adhere to their civilization.

Celia Brayfield was particularly candid about her adult experiences of being 'new' in a field that is competitive at best, and hostile at its worst.

One of the things that I learned, and it's a good lesson for life, is that you are *always* the 'new kid on the block'. The first time you go into school you think, 'Oh my God this is awful. If I'm really nice to everybody, do their homework and carry their bags, then they will have to accept me and I'll never have to do this again.' Wrong – you have to do it again all the time.

I realized that lesson on one of the newspapers where I worked and where I was getting the old bullshit. There's a lot of apprentice persecution in Fleet Street. They use words they think you don't understand, they deliberately don't tell you where things are (particularly the low-grade workers), the secretaries and clerks deliberately impede you just to make it quite clear that they know you don't really belong at 'their' paper.

I walked into that when I was in my late thirties and a senior columnist on Fleet Street; I thought 'this sort of atmosphere is obviously going to go on forever'. At one point in my career, I was a temporary secretary for quite a long period, probably a year, and one of the things you learn very rapidly in that is that there are some offices you can walk into and say, 'Okay, who do I have to fuck to use the photocopier round here?' and there are other offices where you can't say that and you have to say, 'Excuse me, could you tell me where the photocopier is if you have the time after you have finished your coffee?'

I think picking on someone new is something that is particularly endemic in dying, industrial Britain, which is actually what Fleet Street has been up to now. It's a place full of a lot of people who know that ultimately they are going to lose their jobs, so they act in as obstructionist a manner as they possibly can rather than get out from under the situation.

Jenny Agutter, who moved to Los Angeles to further her career, found being 'the new kid' a refreshing experience. Until she chose to relocate she had enjoyed the protective warmth of her extremely supportive family and the almost unheard of good fortune to get acting assignments without really trying. Something within told her that a bit of independence would be a step in the right direction.

To a certain extent I actually enjoyed the competition of arriving in LA for the first time: the newness of it, at the age of twenty-one. Because of the fact that I was new and it was a fresh start, I was willing to give all of my energy to it and in a funny way, at that time, I really *wanted* to struggle on my own because so much had been handed to me on a plate in the past. I'd been so lucky. I went into films by chance and everything seemed to come my way – 'Walkabout', 'The Railway Children', 'Snow Goose'. All of those things happened by chance and one thing came after another. So going to LA and being there on my own was the first time I had to do something totally on my own. I was determined to make it work; I have always enjoyed a little bit of a fight.

Prue Leith was 'the new girl' when she was appointed to the Board of British Rail and like the other women who became 'new' well into their adulthood, learned that being misunderstood or underestimated can be a drag. Sitting in her Kensington office, she laughed openly as she told me about her most intimidating experience as 'the new kid'.

When I joined the Board of British Rail I was the youngest member, and the only woman present, and the only woman they had ever had on the Board. The whole thing was utterly terrifying – I sat on the Board not saying anything in the meeting with sixteen men – half of them titled or with letters after their names and they terrified me. One of the nicest – Sir David Serpell, an ex-top Civil Servant – later wrote me a postcard saying, 'If you want to understand the intricacies of the British Rail management structure you will find a diagram of the matrix on the back of this postcard.'

I turned the postcard over and it was a picture of Hampton Court maze and I thought it was a wonderful thing for him to do; it made me laugh. But at the beginning the men used to stand up when I came into the room. So I had to train them not to stand up, not to keep treating me with such delicacy, and also not to treat me as a dumb blonde. They'd say things like 'If Prue can understand it then anyone can.' Eventually they came to learn that I had more in common with them than they thought, but they had to be taught.

Although Audrey Slaughter didn't change cities or countries, she did get 'the new kid' treatment when her career moved from magazines to newspapers.

Both the newspapers I worked for – *The Sunday Times* and the *Independent* – were very different. Both times I had a reputation as a journalist so it didn't matter, but I had to adapt from magazines to newspapers and they are very different, there's no question about it. On *The Sunday Times* in particular, people were waiting for me to fail. I think the thing to do is get your head down and get on with your work and not show off – not say 'I'm great' – in the end they respect you for your skills and see you are not a nasty person and it comes round.

Member of Parliament Emma Nicolson approached the subject

from a different vantage point and, as one might expect from such a plucky lady, focused on the benefit – rather than the disadvantage of being new. She was the only woman I interviewed who recognized the fact that we are fortunate to be able to *choose* to change our environment.

> Certainly when you travel widely, work in a number of different companies, or when you try different careers, you spend your life adapting to other people's lifestyles and customs. I do it from choice, because if you stay in your own little narrow band of life, a lot of learning is lost to you and the fascination, diversity and humanity of human beings of different customs is lost to us.
>
> I think life is far, far too short to experience and learn and see everything. Now that's a very different situation for us because it's a situation of choice. How different from, say, the refugees I saw on the Thai border. They have great dignity, they are adapting to their lifestyle, living in a refugee camp. So it's fine for me in a free society to make the choice to adapt and learn and adapt again but the reality must be very, very different if it is forced on you because of the need to escape. It is different, totally different for us, because we live in a free society as opposed to being in chains.

Moving to a new environment – even as an adult – can be an intimidating experience, as Sally Burton learned when she and her husband moved to Hollywood. As the 'new wife' to a world-famous actor, she felt scrutinized and anxious for approval. Remembering those days, she told me:

> When I got into the celebrity situation, when I was new to Hollywood, I think I was desperately keen for people to like me. I became more keen for people to like me because I was aware that I became more visible and that is when I started to make mistakes. I wanted everyone to like me and I didn't go with my gut instinct, but now I have learned. New places don't throw me that way anymore.

Lady Porter told me that she'd literally been the 'new' and 'different' kid from a very early age. As she remembers it:

> When I went to boarding school (you have to understand that

England has changed quite a bit) because of the war I was nine years old. It was a school that was kind of like Roedean but was called The Warren and is now closed; it was like a poor imitation of Roedean.

I had to adapt from being a very happy child at home to suddenly being thrown into a revolting boarding school atmosphere. It was at the time also when England was anti-semitic and my name was Cohen so I came up against anti-semitism for the first time. So there was the adaptation from home to being away in a nasty atmosphere, and into bullying. So it was a testing time and, for reasons that I'm not certain of, I've never been somebody who's able *not* to be noticed in a crowd. Even if I don't open my mouth, I can't be not noticed and I can clearly remember saying, 'Why don't you leave me alone, I'm not even doing or saying anything.'

There have been other enormous leaps for me; the county golf scene was something quite different; becoming a magistrate, was again quite different; now civic life. As a child it's difficult because you don't know what to do, but basically I think what you have to do is work out what the scene is, as soon as you can. You get advice immediately. I've always done that. I've always found that most people will tell you anything if you ask them. Most people are happy to talk about things, so you need to get someone – you need to trust them, but you can get free advice all the time. You must know the scene, you've got to know it backwards so that you have – as near as you can – learned what you're liable to get and then, if you make a mistake, you learn by it. You must make mistakes, watch other people, and don't open your mouth too quickly.

Fay Weldon also said she's had plenty of experience of being 'new'. She told me:

I went to fourteen schools as a child. I was brought up in New Zealand as an English girl and then I came to England and I was a New Zealand girl; I spoke a different language and I came from a different culture – wherever I was. This is a very good experience for people and it's probably why I have always adapted. My advice is to just enjoy it; seeing as you have no option, put up with it. I think what you do learn is to act. In a way, you learn to go into places *as if* you controlled them or don't care – which went, I think, against my nature. When you're new, you feel there is a spotlight upon you and so you act.

Some women recoil from change because it represents loss of safety and security. But not one of the women I interviewed felt that being 'new' was harmful to them. It can be disruptive or painful – on a temporary basis – but the benefits in terms of expanded horizons, self-knowledge and increased confidence last far beyond the discomfort and disorientation of being 'new'.

Life's artificial barriers

Evidently, it's not out of the ordinary for women to believe in barriers that – real or imagined – have constricted their lives. Most of us can name our own phantom road-blocks with the same ease as pointing out to others our figure flaws that onlookers simply don't see.

The only 'flaw' that I have felt limited me or served as a barrier between me and life's nebulous opportunities is a speech condition categorized as a 'lateral S'.

Until I was six years old I assumed that I spoke as distinctly as everyone else. But after my parents moved from Oregon to California I was enrolled in a new school and was, once again, forced to face the judgement of my peers. The leader of this particular playground mafia, a stubby girl with pigtails, asked me how old I was and happily I answered that I'd just turned six. But the word that escaped my first grade lips probably sounded something like 'Ssicth'. This was my first introduction to the terror of schoolyard ridicule and, even today, I can see with painful clarity, Miss Pigtails leading her coterie of friends away with the dismissive explanation. 'You can't expect someone like that to know how to talk the right way. After all, she comes from Oregon.'

I didn't return home in tears, but I did grill my mother, over cookies and milk, about what was wrong with the way people in Oregon talked. My mother waited for me to explain my deep interest in the pronunciation of our former home and then she called the principal of the school, complained vehemently, and saw to it that the school enrolled me in its speech therapy programme to spare me further taunts.

The speech therapy didn't work and I still stumble over sibilant sounds, although I rarely hear my own lateral S unless I'm listening to a taped interview. Then I cringe and ask myself how I ever got the nerve to join the debate team in high school, how my high-school principal ever allowed me to be a graduation speaker, and how anyone can focus on *what* I say instead of *how* I say it.

Somerset Maugham, I once read, trained himself to avoid words containing all the letters he had trouble pronouncing. This re-educated vocabulary kept his 'secret' safe for many years and spared both him and his companions many awkward moments.

My pre-Copernican preoccupation with my shortcomings exhibited itself in a different way. I merely convinced myself that I spoke like everyone else, even though the evidence proved that I had a distinctive fuzziness when it came to S.

If people mentioned it or asked me why I spoke 'that way' I reminded myself of the true unfairness of drawing attention to the things we can't change as opposed to the things we can. And one of the gifts of turning thirty was knowing that it was time for me to relax and accept whatever unique traits I had (good or bad) and get on with life. If a lateral S hadn't stopped me from getting a good education, becoming a wife and mother, or working in my chosen field, why let it sabotage my confidence?

I no longer think of my lateral S as a barrier. Where once I felt it eliminated good things from my life, I now know that it is little more than a rather miniscule speech trait; it makes me a noticeable conversationalist. It's not all that different from naturally strong fingernails or an allergy to nickel. It is just one more part of me and whatever it stopped me from accomplishing was obviously something I didn't really need to accomplish anyway.

Imagined road-blocks appear in the lives of many of the women interviewed for this book. And some of these perceived barriers were not gifts from the fates, but circumstances chosen by the woman herself. Lady Porter's thoughts on barriers are a perfect example.

We met in her modern Westminster flat and discussed various aspects of a woman's life while she waited for her exercise coach to arrive. Tan, trim and bursting with resolve, Lady Porter is a woman with deep feelings, strong opinions and a no-nonsense approach to life.

I think that obstruction comes in various forms. In the world that I am involved in, your own colleagues obstruct you because everybody's out for their own angle. In personal terms, I've probably created a barrier by having married very young. I didn't go to university and I left school very young so I suppose you could say that my barrier was not being trained as I should have been. But in a funny way that has not proved to be so.

Unfortunately, it's been more difficult for me to accomplish what I set out to do, but it hasn't stopped me. I don't have the barrier of a husband who tries to stop me. That can be a woman's number one problem. As far as I'm concerned, if he wasn't going to let me do what I wanted to do, I'd be disappointed. I think the family, home, domestic side are barriers and you are going to be one of two kinds of people; you're either going to be somebody who says, 'Right, I'll run them both together' or 'I'll achieve less than I might, but I'll be happy because I've chosen to put my family first'; if I hadn't put my family first I would be in Parliament now. I took the view that I wanted to be able to achieve something in perhaps a more limited area, but I think you are going to have to be terribly ruthless if you really want to get to the top – something's got to give.

The other barriers are those people who stand against me, when I have a leadership election and people stand against me, my opponents. How do I triumph over them? First of all, I think you've got to be very clear about where you are going and have a good record and be prepared to stand up, and then against them. The other way to overcome the barrier of opponents involves the whole business of getting people to help you, attracting people round you that are 'your' people, are confident in you, and have faith in you. You mustn't forget that people are people. That can be very difficult because you've got to look after everyone's concerns; in political terms, I have to remind myself to be nice to the back-benchers, talk with them, not to ignore them.

Sometimes you're so busy with what you are doing you forget about what people are thinking, so I think you have to concentrate very much on other people and that can be very difficult. Politics demands patience, people skills, communication, taking people along with you so they know what the hell you're up to, and in the end, being very tough. If my opponents are going to fight against me, I'll fight back with the same force. You can't be delicate in this life, you've got to be strong.

The novelist Fay Weldon told me that being female had been a barrier when she was younger. It hasn't, however, prevented her – in mid-life – from getting to the top of her field.

I came from a family that values education and I went to St Andrew's University and got an MA in Economics. I was still barred by being a woman, however, because I would have liked to have gone to medical school. Later on there were certainly various areas, at work, where I would have been paid more and got jobs quicker had I not been a woman, but I'm not sure that it would have done me any good as a human being.

Florist Jane Packer also felt that being a woman – particularly a *young* woman – has at times worked against her. It was hard for her to convince men that she was a serious business woman who was determined to be successful. Reflecting on her early career, she recalled:

I think the one barrier that you have to constantly face is not from women, it is from men (still). I think it is one of the things a woman in business has to learn how to handle, and one of the barriers to cross as well. Where there are lots of men within a company, you have to handle their attitude towards you because it is either, 'Oh Jane, she's so sweet, look at her today,' that sort of thing, or they just don't take you seriously, and you have to put up with all that rubbish and the sexist remarks as you wander out of the room. You could cut them dead if you wanted to but you just have to learn to deal with it.

I started my business when I was twenty-two and in some ways that worked quite well for me with people saying, 'Oh my goodness, look at this girl, she's twenty-two . . .' and yet on the other hand, I almost had to stamp my foot to be taken seriously.

Novelist Pat Booth felt that the English class system had worked against her and, unlike Jane Packer, it was women rather than men who made her most self-conscious about her roots.

My East End background was a big barrier. I think I have overcome it with a modicum of humour. I think you have to be quite light and bright about it and really pretend. The English, especially English women, are adept at cleverly putting you down and you must not be subtle with them.

You just shout back at them, be rather unpleasant and say, 'Listen I will not put up with this.' You can't afford to be too subtle with the English. They're past masters at subtlety.

Arabella Pollen told me that in the fashion world it sometimes seemed that *not* having an East End accent was a disadvantage. In addition to being treated like a 'dilettante designer' because she'd had a comfortable home life and a quality education, she admitted that the fashion business was full of barriers.

I suppose there have been hundreds and hundreds of barriers. At work things have gone wrong, huge debts, collections that haven't done well, staff walk-outs, things that have just gone wrong at the worst time, which you think you would never be able to cope with if it ever happened and then it *does* happen and you find you have to cope. Endless things have really affected me; you just have to get beyond those sorts of problem barriers.

Celia Brayfield prefers to focus on opportunities rather than problems. But she told me that she once found the union hierarchy at the *Daily Express* to be an insurmountable barrier.

The first barrier in my career that I really recognized was when I was appointed Television Critic of the *Daily Express*. The Showbusiness Editor, who has since taken early retirement, was an elderly journalist who objected; because all his buddies were in the union it was made an official dispute. I don't think I did very well in that situation. What I should have done was raised hell, but instead I raised hell when it was too late. I was very much the victim of not having the information.

I am essentially a good natured and straightforward person – it's a great handicap because you never expect anybody else to behave like shit. You put yourself in their place and think 'what would I do?' I think everybody ought to do a CSE in 'Truly Shitty Behaviour'.

Caterer Prue Leith, when first asked about barriers felt that ignorance of business techniques blocked her in many ways. But on further reflection she decided that what could have been a barrier was nothing more than a 'solvable problem'. And that seems like a sensible way for us to approach anything we see as a 'barrier'.

> I suppose the major barrier is that I didn't get myself properly educated and I managed to go into business with no knowledge of marketing, accounting, business studies, management, anything like that. All I knew was how to cook but because it was a small company and I could grow gradually, I sort of acquired some of those skills and found they weren't so essential after all. If you can understand the petty cash book, you can probably understand the balance sheet. What I think I did learn very quickly is that there's an awful lot of things that other people can do much better than me. I have got a good reputation as being a good delegator, but the only reason is that I know the chef cooks better than I do; I know the manager manages better than I do and so on. I'm not an ass, it's not false modesty, it's just plain good sense that I know that you can buy skills.

Barriers didn't bother Leslie Kenton because she believes they are in our lives for a purpose.

> I have always believed that the barriers are gifts because you have a force of your destiny and it's going in a particular way. If you block it, you intensify the force, and I have recently begun to even see evil in the terms of that; that evil is a service of life because evil makes everything that appears to block impossible to overcome, because what it does is strengthen you tremendously. In order for each of us to fulfil our destiny we have to be consciously aware of what we're doing. I see the inner and outer person as having to marry so they become a servant of the soul but a conscious surrender is something that has greater wisdom. How about having no money and three children and I had to earn a living? Through tremendous fear I decided to write because I didn't want to have a nine to five job because I wanted to be with my children. I haven't had a job in my life except for one for three days in EMI Records in Hollywood, during summer holidays.
>
> I'd seen all those people in bowler hats on the train reading the pink paper so I bought the pink paper and wrote ideas for five stories and got in touch with people. I saw the editors and showed them my ideas and they were suitably pleased with them. One of them said to me: 'You are a journalist aren't you, you're

not just a housewife,' and I said 'No, I certainly am not just a housewife.' I owned just one dress and I would have to wash it after I'd done the cleaning in it and then wear it out to work.

The editor said, 'I'd like you to do a four-thousand word piece on the state of the heavy lifting gear industry.' I didn't know anything about heavy lifting gear. I went away, having said yes, and spent two days asking people what heavy lifting gear was and narrowed it down to cranes and trucks and wrote this thing.

I was living in this house that I'd bought with my only money; we had no desk so I sat on the stairs to write this thing with the typewriter on the step above me.

It took me hours and hours, probably three or four days. The anguish and the fear and the anxiety that I went through was horrific but the piece was fine. I didn't do it to prove anything, I did it because I had to. It made me strong.

The gratitude attitude

If I'm not careful, it's easy for me to succumb to bouts of self-recrimination in which I waste loads of time feeling sorry for myself.

With almost professional zeal I can lament the fact that people have been unkind to me, or have misunderstood my needs, or have chosen to focus on my faults rather than my strengths. Building up to a crescendo of self-pity, I then *segue* into how wonderful my life would be (or might have been) 'if only . . .' Because I've had years of practice perfecting this 'woe-is-me' exercise I can devote hours (and sometimes days) to feeling victimized by the ill twists of fate.

Deep into one of these tortuous exercises, a friend tried – without success – to cheer me up. She talked about the forthcoming events she'd planned and about the friends who would come to visit. But I was so mired into what had gone wrong with my life in the past that I couldn't work up much enthusiasm for a future that, I was sure, would simply be a long-playing reprieve of the same story.

That's when my friend forced me to take a good long look at what I was doing to myself. She told me that I was refusing to see the multi-dimensional sides of my life. As she cryptically reminded me, it hadn't *all* been heartbreak, trauma and stress. And she told me that as long as I wasted my time feeling sorry for myself I could expect to do so on my own. Everyone, she reminded me, has troubles, and few people have enough excess empathetic energy to waste on someone who is constantly focused on what's wrong with their lives.

Thank God my friend was so blunt. And thank God she was right! She taught me that it takes no more effort to dwell on what's right than on what's wrong, but it pays a much healthier dividend.

My first husband's mother, who was never particularly over-joyed to have me in the family, used to have a habit that I found particularly annoying. She had five children, each of whom had their individual problems or shortcomings, but to hear her talk of her children (and she was not a taciturn woman) they were all sainted over-achievers who were eternally devoted to their mother. It was as if she had blinkers on that only allowed her to see what she *hoped* was the truth, rather than the somewhat less appealing reality before her eyes.

Because I was young (and envious of her warm total approval of them and her cool critical tolerance of me) I thought she must be a stupid woman not to see what was so obvious to the outside world. But now that I'm older I think she may have been on to something useful.

She knew that focusing on problems wouldn't help whatever difficult situation was at hand. So instead she convinced herself that the desired solution was already a reality. For example, if one of her sons forgot her birthday or Mother's Day, she didn't whinge about being 'overlooked'. Instead she talked about the lovely gifts he'd given her in the past or about the letter she'd received from him the month before and ended by commenting how much he loved her and what a thoughtful son he was.

Her ability to see only what she chose to acknowledge may be a gimmick, but it has served her and her blood pressure well for seventy years.

Focusing on what's right in your life instead of what's wrong can be a useful tool. I prefer, unlike my former mother-in-law, to limit my 'gratitude attitude' to real rather than imagined good fortune, but either way it can be uplifting and reinforcing to accept that things, however bad they may be at the moment, could be worse.

The women I interviewed for *The Self-Confidence Trick* had varied replies when I asked them what they were grateful to have in their lives. Their answers were as diverse as their talents and their individual good fortune.

Family was a common subject, but there were many variations on this theme. Sally Burton told me that she was, 'Immensely grateful for having known Richard and married him. That gratitude is a fundamental part of my life now.'

Prue Leith got absolutely carried away when asked if gratitude was an essential part of her life. Shaking her head, as if unable to comprehend her good fortune, she classified herself as a woman who was . . .

. . . superstitiously grateful, because I have such a good life and I have always had a good life; it is fortunate that I had a happy childhood, my parents were wonderful, I adored my brothers, we had lots of money and we were brought up in the strict way. We weren't spoilt but we had everything we needed – a good education, lovely holidays, nice house and I had a pony when I was twelve – so we had a good childhood and I suppose I'm grateful for that because I think it does give you the security to think you can tackle anything; and then I'm grateful for the luck I've had because it's all worked so well.

I now have in my turn a lovely house, two wonderful children, my own horse and the things money buys; but mostly I'm grateful that my children are healthy and intelligent and happy. I'm very grateful *to* them, to the kids. They have not shed a tear when they've gone off to boarding school, for example. I've never had that agony, they're just wonderful kids.

Member of Parliament Emma Nicolson felt that she had been blessed with good fortune because her childhood had been ideal.

I'm very grateful for having been born into a happy family. It's not something you can choose. You can't choose where you're born or who you're born to. It's pure luck whether you're born in a 44th floor flat in a tenement block – you can't choose. And the sort of family that I was born into gave me space to be me.

Jane Packer told me a very touching story about a casual remark made that helped shape her entire career.

One of the things that I am really grateful for is my father – I remember as a child that one of his favourite sayings was 'the

113

best things in life are free'. He helped me realize that you can drive along a country road and look around you and just see wonderful things. With the kind of things that I work with, flowers, plants, mosses and so on, I quite often think of him saying that to me. Sometimes you can look at a particular flower, one that has lots of detail, and it is so humbling somehow because they are just so beautiful.

There are lots of people that I feel grateful to and sometimes I go through this whole thing of feeling really depressed I suppose, in as much as I don't do enough in return for those people.

Arabella Pollen became wistful when I asked about the role that gratitude played in her life. Her answer was quiet, and obviously heartfelt.

I am really grateful to my parents more than anything because they have had a tough time of it. They are together now but they have been apart and gone their separate ways, yet they have always kept us together as a family.

Lynne Franks emphatically told me that gratitude was a 'very major' part of her life, but became so through a process of spiritual growth.

I am terribly grateful. I offer prayers of gratitude twice a day through the 'Gohonz' (the Buddhist altar script) for everything that I have, every benefit in my life. I chant gratitude for the benefits of my life every single day. I am grateful to the mystic law – to the energy of life – for giving me the life I have. I could have been born to a starving mother with three babies in the middle of Africa. I was born in an affluent society, with a career I could do, a great couple of kids, a great relationship with my husband, and great people I know. When I first started practising Buddhism, I just used to sit at these meetings and all these people used to sit there with all their problems. I got nervous and I used to say, 'Well I have to tell you I haven't got any problems', and I was being very, very smug about the whole thing and then problems did start – my marriage went through a terrible time.

It had always been pretty rocky but I had never been really aware of it, and there were lots of work problems, the pressure of my career and in all the areas I thought I didn't have problems in, Buddhism actually brought it out. The problems had to come out because if they hadn't come out, they would have been festering. Once difficulties come out you can see them and make the necessary changes in yourself.

Audrey Slaughter added a personality trait to her gratitude for the people in her life. Sipping coffee in her book-cluttered lounge, she admitted that she was:

Grateful for my friends and my husband. I think these things are a bonus. I am grateful for being a character that doesn't crumble easily. It will take a lot to make me give anything up, and so I think I'm quite good at keeping my friends.

Novelist Pat Booth's Roman Catholicism is as connected to her expression of gratitude as Lynne Franks' Buddhism is to hers. She told me:

Gratitude is a big part of my life and I try to go to mass every day. I am very grateful – I think my turning point was my marriage. I am very grateful for that and I am very grateful for my children. I have been with my husband for twenty years, which seems to be a kind of turning point, even my friends go back all that time. People whom I care about deeply go back all that time. My husband and I have been together for about twenty years, we split up for about two and a half years in the middle and we got back together ten or eleven years ago and we got married. My son is six and a half and I have a little daughter, Camelia, who's one and a bit. I am very grateful for my family actually more than probably anything else.

Celia Brayfield, with the cheerful cynicism of someone who's spent years on Fleet Street, spoke unhesitatingly of the good things in her life.

I am most grateful for good health – on the whole it means I can wake up every morning smiling. I am grateful for common sense because if you don't have that you are in big trouble and with an awful lot of creative people, it actually seems to have fallen off their chromosomes. I'm terribly grateful for my daughter because in my career what I could not do for me, because of my lack of self-esteem, I have no trouble doing for her. As an example – you know in Fleet Street, they always lose your photograph used for photo bylines; once I had come back from maternity leave, they rang and said they had lost my photograph, would I come in and be re-photographed in time to be ready for the next edition – that meant 8.30 in the morning. I didn't have the nerve to ask my nanny to come in at 8.30, so I said, 'No I am not available at that time in the morning,' and they said, 'Fine'; they looked harder and they found it. Had I not had to worry about leaving my child, I would have had my photo retaken regardless of the time.

But for sheer exuberance, it would have been hard to beat Lady Porter's level-headed appraisal of her life's blessings.

I'm grateful for energy, good health. I'm grateful also for a well-balanced home life and an easy going husband. That doesn't mean that he doesn't need handling, all people do. Grateful for the fact that I have the means to be able to run my own life. I can have help. I think that if I hadn't got it, if I had been born in different circumstances, I probably would have gone out and worked anyway. I think I had to be an achiever – it would have been different, it would have been more difficult. I'm very grateful for having two super children and having tremendous energy and vitality.

Ruby Wax told me that her gratitude was tied up, in a convoluted way, with money. In her words:

I've just found out from my bank that I'm missing a grand. My mother's an accountant and she's very meticulous and knows about stocks and bonds and things that I don't have any brains for at all. Those things just don't make any sense so I have no information at all about it. But, then again, if I had to know about it, I would. It's been a real kind of paradox in my life; the very people who made me feel insecure have given me total *financial* security. I am grateful for that.

Claire Rayner is grateful for her family. About her children she said:

I adore them. I always make a joke that they treated us with amiable contempt; my daughter Amanda said to me, 'You tell us that when you are being unjust, we must tell you, but when you

are being unjust you are in no mood to be told, so we don't.'
They're good kids, very nice people, and I consider myself very
lucky.

Whether we do or don't have husbands, families, friends, or
successful careers, there is always *something* for which we can
gather a bit of gratitude. Can it be an accident that those most
willing to acknowledge their good fortune seem to have the most to
be grateful for?

What goes around comes around

A dear friend in California once experienced a heart-breaking
romantic episode in her life, yet in spite of her real-life nightmare,
behaved with incredible dignity throughout the entire experience.
Engaged to a wealthy man a few years her junior, she learned –
after the church had been reserved, the caterer booked, the
invitations ordered, the musicians hired, etc. – that the man's
mother had threatened to disinherit him if the marriage took place.
My friend accepted his cruel rejection, shed a few tears, and never
mentioned the episode again.

Months later I asked her how she'd managed to stay so
composed throughout a crisis that could have seriously damaged
other women's self-composure. She told me that one of her co-
workers, after hearing of her massive jilt, took her aside for a few
words of wisdom. He gave my friend a hug, assured her that
everything would work out for the best in the end, and then told
her that life had an interesting way of evening out the unjust actions
of those who seem to be in power. 'Remember, my dear,' he told
her, 'that what goes around comes around. The hurt he's given you
will ricochet back on him sometime, somewhere, for some reason
that will probably make no sense to him whatsoever. Your job now
is to put all this behind you and get on with the business of living a
good life. You'll be just fine.'

The co-worker was, to my surprise, right. Up till then I'd never
been one for letting 'fate' mete out justice, because I felt that it was
up to me – or someone more powerful than me – to stop
wrongdoers in their tracks.

I was more comfortable with the idea of someone getting their
hand slapped – immediately – for a wrong, then waiting patiently

for the inevitable karmic retribution. But I revised my thinking when, within three years of my friend's heart-break, her former fiancé lost his job, and broke both legs in a crash that ruined his beloved Porsche . . .

It may have been just coincidence that this wealthy young man was confined to bed for several months with casts running from his heels to his hips, but you'd have a hard time convincing my girlfriend of that. Since her experience, I've been on the look-out for other instances in which people 'seem' (but only seem) to get away, scot-free, after wrecking havoc in other people's lives. Of course, the opposite maxim seems to be equally true: those who make life a little nicer for others often find that something even nicer happens to them – again for 'no apparent' reason.

I asked the women I interviewed if they had been aware of any 'karmic' connections in their lives – either good or bad. Their answers sometimes surprised me.

The author of *Pearls* told me an amazing story of boomeranging bad behaviour.

> I call it the Curse of Brayfield – it's really bizarre but one or two people have done spectacularly nasty things to me. One of them was the man who fired me from my first job in the business. He had been newly appointed as the Editor of this magazine and he was totally unpleasant about doing it. I was standing in front of him, twenty years old, and he had not one nice word to say.
>
> He didn't abuse me or anything but he was just vile. In one month he too had been fired, his wife died in childbirth, his wife's parents had custody of his other children, he had a drink problem and was unable to keep any kind of job together in the business. I think it's very important, I do believe in that principle. On the whole I would hesitate to be wilfully malicious to people, feeling that it would come back.

And designer Arabella Pollen said she thought of this issue as one nearer the Golden Rule.

> I do think that you treat people in a way you expect to get treated yourself and I think if you go over the mark, if you do something bad, I think it comes back on you. I really do believe that very, very strongly and I think if you do the dirty on somebody, somewhere along the line it's going to hit you. I'm sure I have

experienced that, though I can't think of any major incident, but I do believe in that very strongly.

Lynne Frank's involvement with Buddhism has taught her that what goes round really does come round. She told me:

My whole life is based on cause and effect. Of course, I see examples of it in my life all the time. That's how I am able to change. If I hear, for example, that someone whom I've never met is bad-mouthing me, I still have made the causes that have made that effect. I have still, without question, been the one who has created that reaction from somebody – even if it is somebody I didn't know. In every area of my life, I am totally aware that there is no such thing as something just happening out of the blue. That is not what life is about. Life is about – you put out, you get back – whether it was this life or another life. My whole philosophy is based on karmic law.

Emma Nicolson, MP, on the other hand, said: 'I tend to think of it more like an open chain, which means if you help or hurt somebody they then go away and help or hurt somebody else. I think it is an open chain.'

Elizabeth Emanuel was succinct in her understanding of karmic pay-off. Her definition?

If somebody does something bad to you, they always get things going bad for them. It does happen – somebody who treated us incredibly badly was just so evil beyond words; it was somebody who worked with us and made life hell so finally we persuaded them we didn't want to work with them anymore and they left. Now they've just got *loads* of problems. You never have to wreak vengeance on people, it just works out that way.

Novelist Pat Booth told me her story.

A dreadful journalist did something to me which was appalling and wrote an awful piece about my husband and continued to write this in *Private Eye* for about a year. We were going to take the people to court. Eventually the paper and the people who were the prime witnesses, settled out of court. We decided to settle out of court because I said to Garth, my husband, 'I can't continue with this, this is just so revolting.' Of the two prime witnesses, one died in Australia and the other got AIDS. I don't

know if that's karma or what, but it was incredible – isn't it
awful?

Lady Porter also felt strongly that 'the bad guys never win'. In
her experience: 'Whenever somebody's been absolutely beastly
about me, the beastliness has rebounded on them. That's why you
mustn't let it get to you.'

Jane Packer told me that there had been lots of incidents where
she *wished* others would reap what they'd sown, but so far they
hadn't come to fruition.

Brenda Dean, however, had a very tangible example of something working out well as a reward for her willingness to be honest.

A very close colleague of mine approached me and said, 'Are
you going to run for the General Secretary's job?' At the time it
wouldn't become vacant for, I thought, about eight years, but
he didn't agree. He said, 'I'd like to be President of the Union,
but I think you would make a good General Secretary. We could
work well together so why don't we have a deal. If you stand for
General Secretary, but don't get elected, don't oppose me for the
number two job.' I agreed. Later we were having an amalgamation with another union and he said, 'Brenda, I need to
unravel that arrangement I have with you because the people
who want to support me for the election will only do so if I go all
out to get the job. That means I need to stand for the General
Secretary's job.' I agreed, didn't get irritable about it, and knew
that it meant he wouldn't stand against me. But it all became a
tremendous mark on my destiny because all this happened
towards the end of 1981. The amalgamation went through, the
President announced he was going to retire, and had we had the
old original agreement I wouldn't have been able to go for the
job. So I ran for President, and when the General Secretary's job
became free . . . I just reckon I wouldn't be General Secretary
today if he hadn't decided to change what had been our original
agreement, so it's come full circle.

Fay Weldon had a calm approach to the inevitable workings out
of karmic debt. She told me:

I do feel everybody has a karmic pay-off eventually. I don't
think 'reap what is sown' is necessarily true in the financial sense
but you can tell in a way. In old age, by the time people are

eighty, their faces show it. These things somehow seem to take a long time working out.

Leslie Kenton's sense of karma focused on our connected worth rather than on our connected deeds. She told me:

I am a living creature and I value all living creatures' right to life. Whether it's a spider you find crawling, or whether it's a young person trying to do something. You can help and make it possible for them. I experience no difference between me and the spider – we're the same.

Whether you use karmic pay-off to lessen the hurt of other people's cruel behaviour or use it to ensure that your own behaviour keeps you out of trouble, it can help to remember that certain cosmic laws – invisible and unprovable – are working on our behalf.

A little help from your friends

Perhaps because I have been without the so-called 'normal' familial support structure for over twenty years (no brothers, sisters, aunts or parents,) I have relied time and time again on my friends to accompany me through life's challenges.

My friends, to me, *are* my family and I only hope they view me in the same light.

The most challenging times in my life have been immediately following each of my divorces. Because I had, in each case, built a life around a man who enjoyed a certain level of professional success, my life (once he said goodbye) changed drastically. The black-tie dinner parties stopped, the whirl of international travel ground to a halt, and the comfort of having someone's love and support at the end of the day evaporated.

Good friends didn't erase the pain of troubled times, but they did dilute the hurt. Fortunately, I was blessed with friends who were not too busy or too distracted to back their amenable words with useful activity. When I needed help getting my three-year-old son to the hospital for surgery, it was a friend who drove us, waited with me throughout the operation and saw to it that things remained smooth back on the home front. When I'd endured just one too many unpleasant conferences with my son's teacher, it was a friend who reminded me that school marks weren't *everything* (and then mailed me a list of famous men – like Onassis and Henry Ford – who had been disappointing students).

And when I decided to move my little family from Los Angeles to London, it was a cadre of girlfriends (whose ages spanned more than four decades) who helped me decide what to bring, what to store and what to sell in a garage sale.

Few women – regardless of their family structure – manage to get by without the support of friends who are willing to help make life a bit more bearable, because in the good times – and especially in the bad – a friend can make all the difference between giving up and getting ahead.

Shirley Conran told me that the break up of her marriage taught her some valuable lessons about friends.

> When I went through my divorce, my friends were helpful, but I was having such worrying money problems that I found it hard to accept material things from them with good grace. It was too embarrassing knowing that I couldn't reciprocate if they took me out for a lovely meal. So I just stayed at home.
>
> For friends' birthdays I would choose something from the house and give it to them as a gift. Eventually my sons sat me down for a chat and reminded me that it was their home too and they didn't like the fact that I was constantly 'denuding' the house.

Losing a spouse also taught Sally Burton about how helpful friends can be.

> When Richard died the girlfriends that I had here in London were fantastic. I said recently to one of them, 'I can't come back to London, to my old life' and she said, 'But we have *all* changed, you are remembering us as we were but we are all so much further in our careers; we are all achieving our goals.' I thought, 'Yes, I have been too wrapped up in myself.'
>
> They were wonderful; one of them was also a widow and was superb; I think it does take someone who has been through it themselves to really help. Shirley Fonda was fantastic to me and absolutely wonderful; she was a few years further along the road so she knew what was happening to me. I found that it motivitated me to go and see other widows after my experiences.

But the frightening thing is that the farther along the road – and I am trying to put it behind me – the less I actually want to deal with Richard's death and talk about it because it is over; that worries me.

Audrey Slaughter's friends rallied round when her magazine folded. As she remembers it:

When *Working Woman* failed financially my friends were very supportive. A lot of them tried to do their best to get more money to keep it going and they were treated very badly. I think in every case where I have had any trouble of any kind my friends have been absolutely great. I haven't even had to ask them, they just understand what to do.

Emma Nicolson's deafness gave her a unique perspective on friendship.

Almost all my life my friends have made all the difference to me, particularly because I am quite deaf. I've got hearing aids now but before I had them (about four years ago) I was much more cut off, so therefore I was more dependent on my friends than most people are. When you don't hear anything that goes on, your friends are your lifeline so I value my friends and they've been so good to me when I'm stuck; people can be so kind and tolerant.
    Perhaps I see bad sides of human nature when people aren't like that; when you've got a handicap, you see the rough side of people who try to humiliate you or embarrass you or do something nasty.

Lynne Franks has a platonic male friend who helps her stay balanced in trying times.

I think again one's friends are very, very important to help, but again it is generally oneself who pulls you through. I have one very close friend who on any area of my life will always tell me the right thing, put me straight back. With work aggravations, if I phone him up and say about something that has happened at work, then immediately he will not say, 'This has happened because of . . .' Instead he will say, 'Go, sit down, take a deep breath, chant for a few minutes, get in the car and come over' – it just gets me back. The relationship that we have, we have for each other. My husband Paul has that effect on me as well but because we are together so much, sometimes you need somebody from outside who can make you jump back up and calm down, because I do get in knots and I do get in panics.

Facing motherhood as a single woman is a daunting challenge, but Celia Brayfield discovered that her friends made life easier than she'd imagined. As she recalls:

My friends were totally, utterly fantastic when I had my daughter – brilliant. I have never felt so loved, I was in hospital, in the maternity ward at the same time as a very well-known socialite and the nurses came down and told me I had more flowers than she did. The fact that they told me was sympathetic.

People shopped for me, cooked for me. My baby was like pass the parcel, you just couldn't give her to enough people to hold while you did this and that. As it was the first time in my life anyone had been truly wonderful; I just found it a miracle. I also find that with certain exceptions, good fortune is difficult for some people to accept. Oddly enough, it seems that the better I do, the more successful I am, the more helpful people are.

Lady Porter told me of two specific instances where her friends made all the difference.

When my daughter got married very young, and went to live in Israel I felt absolutely dreadful. Every time anyone mentioned her name I was in floods of tears; I really didn't understand why, because you don't when you are depressed, you just don't know what's happening to you. Then I went to talk to a couple of good friends and one of them said, 'Why don't you become a magistrate', and I said, 'How can I become a magistrate?' and he sat down with me, he was a magistrate, and he went over it. He did the forms with me, he told me what to do and he clued me in. I have had friends like that all the way.

When I had a hysterectomy, I had another friend who said, 'Look you must do this, let's work it through.' I have a tremendous support system even though I don't have a lot of time for my friends, I still keep in touch.

Pat Booth relies on her husband these days, but friends are still important to her. She told me:

Before I met my husband, I relied on one of my best girlfriends, Cathy McGowan. I used to get deep depressions and would sometimes hide myself away for three or four days – this was when I had my shops when I was nineteen.

She would actually break the door down and get in. I believe in long relationships. I seldom make new friends and when I do I am very loyal to them. I am an extremely loyal person, again because of my Catholic upbringing and because I am a practising Catholic so I have great strong moral imperatives that I try to adhere to. Basically I only really have friends that go back twenty years. I have friends that I made as a teenager and those people are very dear to me and we see each other a lot of the time. We may not see each other for six months because I have been abroad, but the minute we do, we are close again.

Designer Elizabeth Emanuel doesn't think of her friends as a back-drop for bad times. To her they are essential regardless of what's going on in her life.

I'm really lucky to have friends, people you can just talk to at any time. In times of stress and things, it's great to have somebody who understands, someone you don't see maybe for months and then pick up the telephone and pick up the conversation.

Fay Weldon learned, with her first son, how helpful good friends could be.

When I was very young and had a baby and couldn't manage, my friends were an enormous help. Having experienced this, and understood the value of it, you try to be the same for other people. Really, that is what friends are for – on both sides.

Although Leslie Kenton didn't have a particular incident in which a friend had helped her through a rough time, I like what she said about using intuition to select people who *will* be there when you need them.

I choose my friends in a completely unworldly way – on the basis of if they're beautiful, not physical beauty – I love beauty and love to be near it. When you are with beautiful people, people who are what they are, that have a spirit, it just enriches life and that's the criterion I use. It happens in your heart and I follow

125

my heart. It's the only reliable thing about me and I use my intuition, which is very reliable, and then I use my intelligence to justify what I do from my intuition.

5

Grown-up games

There are several phases of adult life that no woman who wishes to grow can afford to ignore. These include issues as disparate as finances, assertiveness, love and health. Each of us, of course, has a different timetable for reaching 'adulthood'; some women manage to stay little girls well into their dotage.

Part of me still feels like a teenager while another part feels positively geriatric. My coming of maturity arrived at about three o'clock one morning shortly after my first husband married a woman in our neighbourhood whom I had known and liked – although not as well as he had.

In the early morning chill I was forced to accept responsibility for my – and my sons' – emotional, financial and social welfare. There was no one for me to blame or hide behind; I was all I had.

Fortunately, it doesn't take catastrophic events to help us grow up, for turning points can arrive at the least auspicious moment. Each of the women I interviewed seemed totally grown up – yet each also retained a youthful twinkle in her eye. A few of their more thought provoking reflections are included here to show just how many ways women can grow up.

Fay Weldon, a mother figure for transitional women everywhere, told me that growth and sacrifice were inextricably connected. In her words:

It's always seemed to me that nothing in society is achieved without a sacrifice – nothing is for nothing – that's the rule.

If you want change, either in society or in your own life, you have to do something to sacrifice – it may be your peace of mind, money, whatever, but something will go. Or if you are doing something for a community, then some kind of personal sacrifice is required. In extreme cases, it's death, but that is how

127

civilization proceeds. It's almost how evolution itself proceeds – by killing off or disposing of what's failed.

And iconoclastic Lynne Franks made it clear that this era's freedom for women made it possible for her to follow her own rules rather than adhere to standards she doesn't admire.

I am not really somebody who will sublimate myself and I have never tried to pretend to be something I am not. But in a superficial way, there are times when I have to act some different role.

I have had problems that I have created myself by being a loud-mouth, but that is my problem. I don't know what the future holds but certainly looking at the past I would never rather have been born at any other time than 1948, then to grow up in the 1960s and peak in the 1980s.

Lynda Chalker told me that she realized she was grown up when she found herself in a foreign country as a teenager.

I felt like an adult when I went to Germany on my own at the age of eighteen. I didn't speak a lot of German and missed my connecting train in Frankfurt, got to Heidelburg in the middle of the night, called on my digs that had been booked, but was told, 'Oh it's been cancelled, you weren't at the station when you were supposed to be.' I argued my way out of that situation, said it was ridiculous for her to expect me to believe that she had let the room at ten o'clock at night. This experience was all part of development; I remember it clearly today and it happened back in 1961.

Prue Leith's maturity arrived the same time as love. She had devoted years to her business and once it became a success, she was ready for marriage and children. As she explained it:

The formula for a successful business is to have the children very late because they do slow you down. There is no question – children and husbands slow you down like anything. By the time I fell in love and married my husband, who had been married before and was much older than me, I was really ready for children. I wanted desperately to be married, have children, be ordinary, and stop being this freaky 39-year-old single business lady.

Arabella Pollen's 'adulthood' in business came while she was in America. She told me that, in the circumstances, the only thing she could do was act with authority.

> I had a show in New York where every single person in the show walked out five minutes before the show started because they refused to give me an electrical cable for the spotlamps. I said I would call the owner so they said they would walk out. So I called their bluff and called the owner – they walked out, but I finally got them back and they did it.

Lady Porter, as a fifteen-year-old, learned how to stand up for herself while she was in Switzerland.

> After I left school my family didn't know what the hell to do with me, so they sent me to Switzerland, which I hated. I was there seven months and I really didn't learn anything, except how to fiddle my way around – that's a good lesson to learn, how to get the best out of a situation. *Never* accept that you can't do it, *never*.
>
> There's always a way even though people are always telling you you can't – you must keep on saying 'Yes, I can'. I was only fifteen and we went on a train and we had to travel something like two days. We were a crowd of school kids, and I asked 'Where do we sleep?' and they said there was nowhere to sleep and we had to just sit there, and I said, '*I'm* not sitting', and I was sure there were *couchettes* on the train. I got the girls and we gave the railway staff a few bob and we managed to sleep on *couchettes*. I think I've always known not just to accept things and how to find my way around. There's always a way and I think that's what you have to learn. It's very important, never accept.

Ruby Wax's growing up came when she was ready to take what she'd learned in intensive therapy and cope as an adult without regular sessions.

> I used to see my therapist because I was in a hole of depression, but since she put her little wand to work, the depressions aren't ever that thick any more. I've learned that now my mood relates to what's happened and usually there's an answer to it now rather than in something that happened twenty years ago, or in the feelings of my inadequacy.

129

Ruby Wax didn't feel like an adult until she'd left her twenties behind her. As she told me, 'It's only in your thirties that you get a feeling of where you stand.'

Leslie Kenton felt like a grown up after she had already become a parent herself.

> After my second divorce I fasted for three weeks – the first time I'd ever fasted – and I went soon after to a monastery in Scotland and I meditated. I had made the decision that there was no going back on it no matter what. Luckily I had $5,000 that my grandfather (my grandmother's third husband whom she had divorced) had left me; it was all the money I had in the world. I refused to take money from my husband because I didn't feel it was right, so that's how I became a journalist, and how I became a responsible adult.

Brenda Dean said that feeling adult was a gradual process. 'I can't say that there is any particular point; I suppose like most people I matured through the knocks that life gave me. I think that I have been lucky that I have not had many.

Claire Rayner's early years, which included the Depression, the Blitz and the Second World War, forced her to cope with adversity at an early age. She not only grew up quickly, she inherited a philosophy of life that, so far, has served her well. 'I have a theory that life will go bad at some time because there's no way your life can be serene all the time. My first twenty years were bad, but the rest have been smashing; I hope they will continue to be good.'

Money

Only within the past year have I pin-pointed my many financial problems. The first stems from what we, in America, call 'math anxiety'. This term is used to describe the problems that young girls have in the classroom when it comes to wrestling with the multiplication tables, algebra, geometry, etc. The theory is that females have an inborn talent at the 'feeling' skills and a rumoured deficiency in the 'objective' subjects.

In my case there was no rumour; it was fact. If I could write or talk my way around a problem, I'd find a grey area large enough to get me a good grade. But faced with problems that only had right or wrong answers, I was hopeless. And, in my school background, those sorts of problems were nearly always found in maths class.

The result was that I grew up into a relatively literate women who had a deep and abiding distrust and dislike of numbers. Numbers were – and are – a source of great discomfort. Unfortunately, money *is* numbers, which helps explain why I have an overdraft in perpetuity, a bank manager with a bleeding ulcer, and a chronic cash-flow crisis.

My first husband – can you believe it – is chairman of the board of a bank. He actually enjoyed balancing the monthly bank statement and computing the accrued depreciation schedules on our property investments! To me, money has been a means to an end (like a trip to the hairdressers, a holiday in California, or a beautiful new blouse). I do not understand appreciating or acquiring money for its own worth. Or I didn't until last year.

Up until then I'd been content to live *as if* I had money. If I *seemed* to be affluent it was enough. But some chronological watershed visited me and since then I've realized that I cannot creep into old age carrying a knapsack full of financial worries on my back. I *must* grow up and get my monetary affairs into order.

Oddly enough, I seem to be in good company when it comes to handling the really important financial issues and failing miserably with the small ones. I've managed to purchase my own home and raise two sons without any signs of glaring need or negligence, but do not make the mistake of assuming that I have the taxi fare home in my handbag because chances are that I don't.

This ability to handle – if only by the seat of one's pants – the crucial financial issues, while failing miserably with the mundane monetary concerns, is not limited to yours truly. Far better, wiser and richer women than I seem to experience the same 'easy come, easier go' attitude towards their finances. If you do not read the *FT* for hot tips, worry about your stocks and bonds, or keep your bankbook balanced, you are not alone. With relief, I will now introduce you to a gallery of women who may seem to be financially astute but who are, like me, simply lucky.

Shirley Conran, who has gone from the penny-pinching status of an unemployed divorcee to the prosperous state of being a best-selling author laughed when I asked how she felt about money. With a chuckle she told me, 'All that I can say is that I have a personal budget and a business budget, but I never stick to either one of them.'

Fay Weldon admitted:

It's very much the same for me. I think it tends to be that some people are born with the ability to handle money, and are organized, no matter how much they earn. Others always manage to spend more than they have, which in the end can become quite difficult. Because I require the anxiety of money in order to work you can tell which group I belong to. I do have a husband who earns well but with children there are always expenses going out on them.

Emma Nicolson, who doesn't seem to have a vague bone in her body, said that she was not particularly meticulous when it came to money.

I'm pretty vague on the subject – I've always worked on the principle that if I haven't got enough money, I must go out and get a job that pays more but it is not an attitude that my bank manager likes. So far it has worked, because I have been lucky enough to be well paid when I worked in computers, then I went into my job with the Save The Children Fund, which was very badly paid, obviously, because it was a charity. I don't give a lot of thought to money until I don't have any.

Sally Burton told me that she has a schizophrenic approach to her finances. As she explained:

I have two attitudes to money – neither of which is a professional approach because I am not running a department and respons- ible for an expense budget – but I find there is Richard's money and then there is my money, the money I earn; they are two different things.

When we were married I used to feel so bad about spending his money, but he didn't give a damn. In fact, I once suggested to him that he give me an annual allowance, and that I would manage within that budget rather than use charge cards and accounts for all those things that one is encouraged to have and cause you to lose track of what you are spending. I used to get terribly panic-stricken but he thought it was terribly un- necessary; but if it was going to keep me quiet, he probably would have gone along with it.

Lynne Franks, like most of the women I interviewed, didn't feel that the idea of money was particularly appealing. Her approach, as one might expect of her, seemed honest and forthright.

I don't value the idea of money but I do value the idea of financial success and I do like what money brings. I think it is because we like it too much. I am terrible about money – I lose money, I lose cheques. I have to be kept away from it. I am very, very disrespectful to money and I also can be extremely extravagant and have to be controlled and be lectured and told off constantly by my husband, accountants and friends. To be perfectly honest, my husband does our accounts.

I am personally irresponsible, but I am professionally very responsible. We have to look after clients' money and with that I am very responsible, honest and honourable. I will also give away to friends. For money is there to enjoy and use and give out, give away and spend and whatever you feel like doing with it.

I am also a socialist and would pay more tax if money went to the right people and I believed it would. I am confident enough in my own abilities that I can go out and work harder and earn more and I am still only just at the pinnacle of where I am going to and I am more than happy to give money back; I am not unique in this. I realized that there are an awful lot of people who are running successful businesses but also want to do something to help other people. People become so mercenary in business; in this company we spend a lot of time taking charge of projects that we believe in regardless of the money.

Lady Porter had the good fortune to grow up in an affluent household. But she told me that she still has . . .

. . . a rather peculiar attitude towards money. I've always had money that my father made, but I have a tremendous respect for money; even to this day, my children will say I've got the most peculiar attitude to money. Some days I won't buy anything because it's too expensive. Because we're in the grocery trade, if I go into a shop and I want to buy some fruit and I think, 'God I'm not paying that price', I will cut my nose off to spite my face because I won't buy it. I'll walk out and wait and buy it from one of our stores. I don't know why it is, but I cannot throw money away in that context. On the other hand, I can go out and spend money on things without even thinking about it. I'm a mixture – one day I'm very careful and the next I'm not. I never carry money. I never have money on me. I'm like the Queen. I'm not somebody who walks around with plenty of cash; I don't have a casual attitude, it's a mixed attitude.

Leslie Kenton, who looks very prosperous, is as muddled about money as the rest of us; her 'professional' ego seems almost non-existent.

If people ask me about my career, I just laugh because I've never thought of having a career in my life, all I've ever done is to cope and manage to pay the milk bill and have fun doing it, but I'll take it all seriously. I think now is the first time in my life that I have chosen in the sense of deciding what to do. What I've now done is said, 'I know I have to do this,' and it's a very different thing from what I did before. I am completely naïve about the world, I don't know how it works. I have never in my life been to a party, dinner, anything in order to further a career – never because I would get bad tempered and be unpleasant to someone.

I worked for the National Magazine Company for fourteen and a half years, it was a Hearst company and I had a little contretemps with the managing director who wanted to own my copyrights (I was the only one in the company who owned all the copyrights). I had to write a letter saying I'd be happy for them to have my copyrights but naturally they must understand that because they were mine, etc., etc., etc. And I wound up misspelling 'Hearst' because I never bothered to learn how to spell it; and someone said that was the most honest expression of contempt they'd ever seen in their life. But I didn't even know I'd done it and that's how naïve that I am about the way things work.

I don't really want to know about money or power or career strategy. I just want to do what I want to do. I believe that if you try to do what you want, that God will look after you. If I didn't, I'd be in trouble because there's no way I can look after myself.

Prue Leith discussed her personal and professional approach to money with humour-filled candour.

I'll go to a dress shop and spend £1,000 in an afternoon buying four outfits, all much too expensive, but then I won't go shopping for a year and I will suddenly find myself incredibly mean about a pair of socks and I will darn them instead of ditching them. I have stages of incredible meanness but I think I would certainly say my attitude towards money is that it is lovely stuff – the more of it the better and financial success is important but mainly it is important because it is the yardstick by which you are judged. If you run a business, it is no good if it is the best food in town if you are not making money because you know that actually, you are being a failure – it has got to be profitable.

It gives me great pleasure to run a profitable business. Sometimes I will nurse an unprofitable part of the group along for a while because I believe it will come round or because I believe it is doing tremendous good to the rest of the group. For example, we might have courses at the cookery school, wine courses, but they are not particularly profitable – wine costs a lot of money and you can't charge a lot for wine tasting – but it is terribly important for our image that we don't want to just be a cookery school, but a school of food and wine. I would not like it at all though, if we lost a lot of money.

Jane Packer, who didn't grow up in a wealthy household, said that money was nice, but job satisfaction was nicer. She told me:

I like nice things, I don't think I'm either particularly extravagant or frugal. It is only within the last eighteen months within my company that I have earned anything near a proper wage, because before that the money had to go back into the business.

There have been lots of weeks that by the time I had paid off everybody else there was nothing left for me. That's the thing that people don't seem to realize. When I have the money, I tend to buy myself something nice, or if I have worked particularly hard, then I will treat myself to something. But money is not the most important thing to me at all. I think the respect I get from the work I do is more important.

With a beautiful home in Florida and a series of best-sellers, Pat Booth has earned a wealthy lifestyle. But as she explained, she is not a financial wizard:

I don't have a particular awareness of money. I work exclusively – and have always done so – to prove things to myself. I am told that I have made a lot of money but I feel deeply insecure financially and always will. Money doesn't bring me emotional security at all.

I always have 'plastic', I spend far too much and then get really mean with buying washing powder and I want two pence off – things like that – I get really mean at times.

Arabella Pollen, who exudes an aura of never having a care in the world, told me that the science of money management is a mystery to her. As she explained:

My money just goes everywhere. This is entirely my husband's fault because he is probably the most generous man I have ever met in my life. If he's got no money then we go without for the week, but if he's got money, it's spent on champagne and salmon and he gives me a £50 note and says 'spend'. He just spends money like water when he has it and since he is a survivor, I don't worry about it; he is a great horseman and likes the horses, he can be a great gambler.

I'm used to having either nothing or a windfall. If it's there, it's gone and if it's not there, you have to get by on what you've got.

At work I'm pretty bad as well. The financial side of the business is dealt with by my brother. I think that it's very important that the financial and the design sides fight all the time because they are actually opposites and if you find a controller and a creative person getting on well, there is something wrong. I always want more money, I always want bigger budgets and he always fights that tendency, which is how it should be; it keeps a balance.

Some people, like Celia Brayfield, are lucky enough to change their attitude toward money. She told me that her approach has shifted 180 degrees during the past few years.

Money was the major area of reconstruction. I had a concept of being an artist; I saw myself as an artist which I think a lot of people in journalism don't. I saw myself as someone who was only interested in creativity and ought to be starving. The major contribution of attending a Success Unlimited Seminar was just simply having someone lead me up to the top of the hill to let me see that attitude and what it meant when spread out. What I had to do was turn round and say, 'But that's rubbish'.

I was asked 'How do you feel about people who are absurdly rich, think of the millionaires you know, how do you feel about them?' I answered, 'Well, they're nice people', and was told, 'People might think that about you if you were one.' It's very British to be embarrassed about being rich and successful.

You do have to be careful and self-effacing because people are very funny about it. If you have the confidence you can say, 'Yes, this outfit cost me £400, it really suits me. I really like it, I hope you do too'. But I wouldn't do that; I'm far more likely to say, 'Oh I just picked it out.'

Brenda Dean told me that her *laissez-faire* attitude towards money was probably due to her need for a contrast from her highly organized attitude towards work.

I take great pride in doing the administrative side of my job well. I know all the facts and figures about our union, yet in my own life I continually lose my car key and my house key. I certainly don't know how much money is in my bank account at the moment, so without doubt I am totally disorganized when it comes to my private financial affairs.

And Elizabeth Emmanual told me that she wasn't an extravagant person but did feel that money was important, particularly so the children could have nice things. In her words, 'I never have cash in my bag and I must say I am not brilliantly organized about that, but we *are* organized in the business sense.'

I don't mind admitting that I'm as 'disorganized' about my everyday finances as most of the women in this book. And, like Celia Brayfield, I am far past the stage of imagining myself as someone with principles too high and lofty to be tainted by filthy lucre. I like the things that money can provide, but I'm afraid I will always get a bigger thrill out of *doing* what earns the money, than manipulating and multiplying the money itself. At least I'm in good company . . .

Assertiveness versus aggressiveness

It took a three-year time span for me to learn how to differentiate between these two expressions of power. For years, whenever I was threatened or felt angry, I behaved aggressively. This tendency to over-react boomeranged back on me with predictably unpleasant results.

The first time in my thirty-odd-year life that I exhibited real, constructive assertiveness came last year. My boss wanted me to be present for a meeting with a prospective employee who was applying for an important position in our firm. I'd already interviewed the gentleman in question once but my boss insisted I attend a second meeting; acceding to his request would have involved reneging on a previous commitment. Three months earlier, I had been invited to a *very important* luncheon and had accepted with glee. It would be an opportunity to meet Sir Geoffrey Howe, several ambassadors, and enjoy the hospitality of a highly respected Member of Parliament whom I liked and deeply admired. I had told my would-be host months before that I would be at his luncheon, without fail. Yet now I was being pressured by my boss to cancel my arrangements.

Had I been younger I would have cancelled the lunch, held a long simmering grudge against my boss for 'making me' miss the affair, and then, at some inopportune moment (long after my boss had forgotten my rearranged plans) expressed my anger and disappointment in a hostile and inappropriate manner.

But this time, I stood my ground. I explained to my boss why this luncheon, and the host, were important to me, I reminded him of my deep commitment to finding the right candidate to fill the vacancy at our firm and I volunteered to meet boss and applicant either the minute after my lunch finished or else before it began. I made it emphatically clear, however, that I had no intention of breaking an important commitment I had made months earlier.

Oddly enough, this assertive stance worked perfectly. My boss was puzzled, but accepting (possibly because he knew I was *not* going to change my mind); my host was pleased that I hadn't ruined his seating plan; I felt thrilled to satisfy my obligation to both my host and my boss; and I managed to be at the slightly rescheduled applicant interview on time. Best of all, I wasn't angry with anyone afterwards.

This is a distinct improvement over the times when I felt 'forced' to do something I didn't want to do and then felt compelled to 'punish' the person in power.

That sort of aggressiveness hurt my peace of mind, my career, and my relations with people who couldn't understand why I had such an 'inappropriate' level of inner anger. The only thing I can say in my defence, is that at least my aggressive behaviour was reactive rather than spontaneous. But that's not much of an excuse.

The same lessons I've learned about curbing my aggressiveness have been shared by the women in this book. But each of their stories, although different, have all reached the same conclusion: it simply doesn't pay to be aggressive. Assertiveness can get you exactly what you want and it has a much more acceptable price tag.

Sally Burton has learned to stand up for her rights rather than be told by others what to do or think.

> I think one does benefit from being assertive. It helps your own peace of mind by being assertive and saying, 'Yes it is what I want' – the balance is that you will be accused of being aggressive anyway and other people will be upset. At the end of the day I would rather be happy with myself than kicking myself for being so wet and going along with someone else's idea when instinctively I knew it was incorrect.

And Lynda Chalker told me:

> I think it is dangerous for a woman to be over-aggressive (this will sound strange to you if you know the House of Commons). You can be firm, but if you constantly deride other people, then you are not actually respected. You have to be able to demolish a case, without demolishing a person; men can get away with being physically and verbally aggressive – I don't think women can succeed in the same way.

Detta O'Cathain told me of her experience with both assertiveness and aggression.

> I've certainly benefited in my career by being assertive. My very first breakthough into the upper echelons came because I was assertive; I saw a job advertisement in the paper, which specified a male and I said, 'I've got all the qualifications apart from the fact that my gender is wrong.' And that was thought to be assertive. Maybe that was a breakthrough – my whole career has benefited from being assertive.
> I try to be assertive but there are occasions when I lose my rag. I think the Irish in me comes out and I lose face by that, but

when I think about it, the couple of occasions when I have really loathed myself for losing my temper has been in the home environment with my husband. Over a long period of years it's inevitable, but I hate that when it happens – I really hate it because you say things that are much better not said.

I do remember a situation where I totally lost my temper with a secretary, and it still bugs me even though I know I was right. This must have been about ten years ago I would think. The real problem was she was not capable. I had agreed to employ her because she was black and I thought she ought to have a chance. She was a charming girl, pleasant to have around and she was just very nice.

She was loyal and could be trusted, but then she had this streak in her, probably from coming from a disadvantaged section of the population. She could be absolutely dogmatic that she was correct. She pointed out that in a letter that I had dictated I had said such and such, which was totally wrong, there was no way I would have said such a thing. There was no way I would have used the expressions, there was just no way – my English is grammatical, yet she would say, 'Well you dictated it, you definitely dictated it.' She was obviously covering up for the fact that she wasn't taking her dictation that correctly and she wasn't prepared to admit it. I put up with that week after week, but on one occasion when she was particularly stubborn, I absolutely flew at her. I didn't physically fly at her, but verbally I absolutely chopped her in small pieces.

Fortunately I didn't make any references to her ethnic origins or anything like that, I was just furious with her sheer incompetence. What I was really getting at, of course, was myself for being stupid – I know that I had been irresponsible to employ her. Not that she shouldn't have been employed, but she should have been employed in a more junior position where there weren't the pressures of somebody as busy as me who relies enormously on a secretary. I'd foolishly taken her out of a typing pool situation where she could paint her nails in between doing a few letters and put her into a situation where she was pressured. I think she couldn't cope with it, therefore my anger at her was the effect of the sheer anger at myself for doing it. I really hate that sort of aggression – she probably forgot it years ago, but it is vivid to me even today; it was a great lesson – it taught me never to do it again.

140

Prue Leith told me:

Yes, I certainly think I have benefited by being assertive. I learned on the British Railways Board that I'd better speak out and be a bit of a bully or else nobody would take any notice.

For example, I had to fight very hard to get British Rail to take any notice of women in management. We were supposed to be an equal opportunities employer, but that just meant we had signed a bit of paper. There was no real commitment and everybody, although they all thought they were so unprejudiced as anything, was incredibly prejudiced. I had to really force them to listen to me and I became quite boring about it and was teased about being a burning feminist, but I think that paid off because they did listen.

I think one example of being hurt by my own aggression is that the manager of our restaurant for years, who is a very good friend, is just leaving because he has run the restaurant for fifteen years and he is tired of it and wants to do something else. One of the reasons he is tired, I reckon, although he hasn't been so mean as to say so, is that I'm very persistent and if we disagree over how things should happen, I would be very polite and say, 'Well that's interesting, but. . .' and I never give up. One day he walked out of this office in an absolute fury. He left me in floods of tears and he was in tears as well and we had to kiss and make up because we had argued about where a drinks party should be held. I felt that he didn't want it to be in the bar because it would be a nuisance to him, and I thought he ought to start thinking about what the customers would like and I said to him, 'It won't be much of a problem, I promise we will move them out in time.' Then he suddenly said, 'Well I don't know why I bother to argue with you because you will always get your own way in the end. You are the most impossible bully. . .' and off he went, twelve years of frustration of working for me having tumbled out. I was absolutely appalled because I didn't realize I was quite so aggressive.

Pat Booth, who looks too delicate to be either assertive *or* aggressive surprised me with her thoughts on this subject.

I think women actually have to be more assertive than they wish to be; because of that you have to be quite sure of the sort of man you are going to marry because you have to have tremendous support from that man, since the rest of the world is basically your enemy.

You have to go out there and fight, and many times Garth has heard me complain (I'm very demanding where my work is concerned) and he has said to me, 'You can't do that. You mustn't say that, you're going to blow the whole thing' – and I don't care.

Basically, at the end of the day, all I want is my own way. If somebody asks me what I want, it is my own way. As long as my work is tackled and dealt with I am as happy as Larry and very easy going. But if my work is not dealt with that way, then I'm not, so I'm *very* assertive and I feel that women have to be more aggressive than they actually are – even if it means it makes them unhappy at times.

Although I've never thought of the fashion world as a place that calls for particularly assertive behaviour, Elizabeth Emanuel told me that strength and power are very much part of the world of style.

I think it is very important to be assertive. It's incredible how you can sway people if you have the confidence, if you do it once then it builds up your confidence. It is important, if you sit there and hunch up and look nervous about something, people don't have any respect for you. There is a borderline between assertion and aggression, when you become really frustrated because you can't put a point across. I know I have got a lot harder, I never used to be as tough as I can be now. Usually I'm not but I can be frustrated when I've got something I'm trying to do and there are hurdles in the way. I try to be more assertive than aggressive, but in times of tension then it's very difficult and that's why you have to have understanding people around you.

Jane Packer, who seems rather shy, told me of a recent experience with aggression during which her shyness evaporated.

I find it very hard to assert myself, but it depends on who the people are. There are some people that I can walk in and really pretend that I know exactly what I am talking about, what I am doing, really control the situation. Yet nine times out of ten, I tend to let those people, and the situation control me slightly.

But then every so often, if I see that somebody is abusing the fact that I am quite willing to let them lead the conversation and take control of the situation, if I see that they are abusing that, then I get assertive.

I was once out with a friend and we went together to the launch party of a magazine. She's very successful in her career and well respected amongst these people and she knew almost everybody in the fashion circuit. I only knew one or two people, and as we were walking round instead of introducing me by saying, 'This is Jane Packer', she would say to them (because about three weeks before I had done the flowers for her wedding), 'Oh this is Jane, my flower girl.' I stood there for about half an hour just listening to this and I was really boiling.

There was no need for it. I was so angry and in the end I just sort of exploded. I knew I was right and I was glad that I did it because she was behaving disgustingly. I said to her, 'I really think I should be wandering round with a basket over my arm flogging flowers for £2.00 a time.' Because of who she is and what she is, I was quite happy just to be there watching her life, but as soon as that happened, I had to get the aggression out of my system.

If I had left and not said anything at all I would have been really cross with myself and with her.

Emma Nicolson told me that she felt assertiveness and aggressiveness could be tied to gender conditioning.

It's taken me a long time to find a balance between myself and being what I originally thought society wanted a woman to be. I have a lot of energy and I think I was brought up to think that women were meant to be seen and not heard. I found that difficult within myself and have thrown that aside because life is too short.

I think sometimes I do get aggressive with people. If it's someone in a junior position you do regret it because you are the boss and you must not do that. It is easy sometimes to get like that when somebody doesn't perform (even though you've persistently told them to work well or have taught them to work well and given them every possible help). Then it becomes very irritating and you can snap and you do regret it afterwards. I've been grumpy with one or two poor-quality staff that clearly could do a great deal better and are being selfish and boring, but I think a level of aggression is in everybody. It's probably quite a powerful way of moving things forward. I don't think aggression is always bad.

Occasionally, I still have trouble knowing when to be assertive as opposed to being aggressive, but confusing the two is less likely to happen when you keep your goal – and the effect of your words – in focus.

Smother love

Although many women find themselves 'smothering' their mate in unwanted attention or unwelcome affectionate demands, the sort of man to tolerate such behaviour was never a part of my romantic reality. Where I did come dangerously close to 'smother love', however, was with my two sons. Without meaning to, I had thrown myself into being a 'Supermom *manquée*'.

Licking my wounds after my divorces, I comforted myself with the adage that 'men come and go, but a child is yours forever'. Foolishly I tried to meet their every need, even when I no longer had the physical, financial or emotional resources to do so. I told myself that as I had no living relatives, my two sons would comprise an oasis of affection and warmth in the desert of my emotional life. Ha!

What happened is that our happy London home became increasingly less happy. My younger son began pining – physically – to go back home to America, and my older son realized that to be a success in the land of his birth he needed to finish his education on the other side of the Atlantic.

It took several months for me to reconcile myself to the fact that there was no one at home to 'smother love'. House-bound because of a health problem, I had lots of time and lots of empty rooms in which to think about the hazards of oppressive motherhood. I had to accept that on the one hand I had physically neglected my sons because of my own ill health, while on the other hand I had expected them to give me a psychological reinforcement that few adults would have been strong enough to shoulder.

I cried for several week, tortured myself by looking at old photo albums of our 'happier' life together, and generally did a lot of

Marilyn-bashing before I realized that the love between us hadn't been altered – just the expression of those feelings had been changed. I couldn't ask them, at the end of the day, what had happened in school. But I could write and let them know that I cared about their scholastic progress. The distance between us – over 6,000 miles and eight time zones – forced me to quit focusing on them and broaden the scope of my own world

Each of us, at some time, must let go of the person or people we love. For those of us inclined to emotionally wrap ourselves around someone else (perhaps like me, in order to bolster our flagging sense of lovability) it can be a difficult break. But knowing that love is love – whether it's conveyed with smothering attention or a light touch – helps keep the connection open instead of oppressive.

The women I interviewed seemed pretty divided when it came to the issue of how they loved. Some admitted to 'smother love' while others were adamant that they preferred love with a light touch.

Elizabeth Emanuel felt that her ethnicity and the zodiac were to blame. In her words:

> I'm Cancer and Jewish so you get a really bad intense Jewish-mother syndrome, which means you tend to smother people automatically and I think I probably do. You know, an over the top, homely sort of thing.

Audrey Slaughter admitted that she had smother loved and paid a penalty for doing so.

> I think probably I was rather possessive with my son. My daughter is a different temperament so it didn't matter so much with her. I tried to tell my son what to do with his life all the time; there was a very painful estrangement, which was extremely upsetting, he just wouldn't talk to me and I didn't know what was going on. I found that very hurtful, but I think it was probably my handling of it.

And Arabella Pollen, who has the quasi-ethereal looks of someone who would *never* be possessive told me that in her marriage smother love is alive and well.

> I wouldn't say that I loved with a light touch. You can't love a Latin person (and my husband is Italian) with a light touch, it doesn't exist. I don't think you can quantify the amount you

love, I don't think you control that very much. Having said that, you still have to employ feminine wiles to keep your man, but I think you have to love 100 per cent, I think I would be quite suspicious of somebody who said they were only going to love 50 per cent, I think that's an unnatural thing to do.

Jane Packer admitted that she could be over attentive with her affection if it weren't for demands of her career.

I do tend to be smothery, particularly with people I like or have a particular affection for. If I had more time I could end up being a smother lover, if I didn't have my career and everything because it is very important to me and it takes up a lot of time. I am sure I would be one of those women about whom people think, 'Oh my God, get me away from her.'

Celia Brayfield, who lives alone with her daughter, admits that she has the capacity, if not the intellect, to overpower people with love. She told me:

I'm a Leo. As far as a Leo is concerned a light touch is not love, so I probably smother love my daughter. Actually, I don't think I have done it before. I have only had three serious relationships but I don't think I ever did that to any of them. It was something I knew I *could* do but I really didn't want to do it.

Sally Burton, like several others, didn't feel she'd been guilty of going overboard on being possessive.

I am not aware of smother loving. I must say I gave everything to Richard but I don't think it was detrimental. It was something he needed. So I have not experienced that.

In her customary straightforward way, mother of four Fay Weldon made it clear that she didn't overpower her offspring with unwelcome affection.

All women with children feel guilty about working and think of all kind of reasons they shouldn't – but I don't think for one minute most women would smother love their children. What is smother love anyway? It's neurotic really. Children are so much more resilient nowadays that it is very hard to smother love them. I don't think I suffer from that tendency.

Pat Booth and Leslie Kenton spoke about passion and tried to describe how they were able to love with a light touch but be passionate at the same time. Pat Booth told me:

I love with a light touch. But passion is a bit smothering. I mean when I'm in passion that's completely a different thing for me as opposed to in love. My 'in passion' period becomes very smothering. With my children – no – I allow them tremendous independence from me. I don't want to smother, in fact, I feel it would be pretty unhealthy.

And Leslie Kenton, who had strong feelings about almost everything, told me her feelings about loving, letting go, and love – American style.

I think as a family we respect each other so much. There's always a period around seventeen, eighteen when a child goes through a temporary thing and everything is against the mother, father or whatever. That's part of taking a knife and cutting the connection with the mother which is absolutely necessary for independence and now we are better friends than before. I love the process when parenthood ends and individual human connection begins because then the richness of the relationship is something you don't have as a parent.

As before, if you look at it, it's the only way to be a responsible parent because then you are not asking your children to approve of you and that's what a lot of parents do, and that's wrong. I think people should be adult when they're grown up, not infants. I think men/women relationships in America are so adolescent – they're always falling in love and then they're always disillusioned, etc., it's so boring. I do not find American men interesting or attractive, not at all, they're basically boring.

Lady Porter told me that she doesn't 'smother love' her family because, as a child, she got a taste of it as a recipient.

I love with a light touch – I think you have to because if you smother, you smother the thing you love. You must let go. I think it's hard – no it isn't that hard because if you've been smother loved yourself then you usually think to yourself 'no' and you'll do the opposite. A lot of love and affection, yes, but I think it's healthy to have it counter-balanced by the boarding school bit. When I grew up, it was different days then, girls didn't do anything in those days.

Rather than discuss the issue in an abstract way, Prue Leith told me how smother love works in her family.

I think that I hold off. My little boy is tremendously affectionate – he's twelve – and he is very babyish and my little girl is thirteen; actually, there's only eight months between them because she's adopted. Anyway, she is very independent and grown up but Daniel seems very much the little boy.

When I started protesting about him going to school – he is going to Eton this year – I said to Rayne, 'We can't send him off to Eton because it is not a weekly boarding school and I want him home weekends', and my husband said, 'look, we had exactly the same argument when he was eight and now we are having it when he is twelve, but he will be your darling baby boy until he is forty, so you might as well get used to the fact he is not going to be under your wing all the time.' I sometimes feel that because he is very affectionate and I am very affectionate that I am going to give him some mother hang-up, that he is going to grow up queer or something because he is so devoted to me. We seem devoted to each other so it's too bad, but still at the age of twelve I give him a cuddle in the mornings; if there was a danger of smother loving it would be with Daniel. When he wanted to go to a polo camp with his pony last summer, I thought, 'Great, wonderful, he goes down to some army barracks where they all play around with their ponies for a few days', and I sent him off very bravely. His eyes were full of tears as he was leaving and I suddenly thought 'Poor boy, he doesn't know anybody and he's nervous about whether he will control the pony.' But we both pretended we were fine, we waved goodbye as if we were fine and then, of course, I lay awake all night thinking he would be in Stoke Mandeville Hospital, wondering 'what have I done, he can't ride that pony'. I just got myself into a fantastic state about it, I must have rung my husband ten times the night he was due to come back, asking 'Is he home yet?' And he kept saying to me, 'Look, they stopped playing at four o'clock and it is now ten o'clock at night.' My husband knew he was *en route* home and told me 'If he had been hurt we would know about it by now.'

No chance of smothering Li-Da, our Cambodian daughter. She's too independent.

Your body is only human

It's easy for women with a dream to assume that their bodies are machines designed to obey orders. For some of us, however, the body presents a hurdle that changes not only our goals, but the whole fabric of our lives. The bad news is that it erases our pre-conceived self-image, our 'dependable' good health, and our ability to live a cerebral life without being concerned about the physical side of life. The good news is that a serious illness can transform our psyche, leaving in its wake a wiser, nicer, more thoughtful survivor. And although it's said that medical sagas are interesting only to those who experience them, in this chapter several women share their stories.

Here's mine . . .

Before I moved to London, my job was Health and Fitness Editor for The *Los Angeles Times* Syndicate. Every week I had to compile a collection of articles that were sold to foreign and domestic newspapers. A primary job requirement was to be familiar and up-to-date with the latest developments in health, exercise, diet, beauty, nutrition and behaviour. One of the fringe benefits of the job was becoming friendly with contributors and experts like Norman Cousins, Bruce Jenner and Nathan Pritikin; although I knew I could never hope to be a genuine exercise or beauty authority, it was an unspoken part of the job to act and look the part of a Health and Fitness Editor.

Although I was more an observer than participant when it came to facials or jogging or weight lifting, I did get copious amounts of exercise on horseback. Several times a week, I'd drive to the stables and get a good 'cardiovascular workout', and most weekends I'd compete in hunter jumper-trials.

Years earlier, I'd indulged my desire for exercise (and discipline) through ballet classes. Toe shoes and tights were an integral part of my life, but at age twenty-five I changed my allegiance to horses – an object of flirtation since childhood.

So as 1984 began, I was an extremely fit female according to my annual check-up; my cholesterol and weight were the same number, my exercise oxygen capacity readings were well above average, and my blood sugar and blood pressure levels were both normal.

But 1984 was not a particularly good year for me. I went through my devastating second divorce, my editor at work sent me home from the paper with tears in my eyes more times than I could count, I lost fifteen pounds in two weeks, I found myself waking at three in the morning on a regular basis (always a danger sign for me) and I was full of concern over demands connected with my official equestrian hospitality role in the upcoming Summer Olympics. Pressure, stress and low-level depression were becoming constants in my mental life; soon they affected my physical well-being.

My saga really began when I decided – before the 1984 Summer Olympics – to have overdue surgery to get my ballet-damaged toes repaired. Years of pointe shoes had slowly ruined my toes so that wearing even ordinary footwear had become an uncomfortable proposition. The Olympics, I knew, would be torture unless my feet could withstand long hours and lots of walking. But forty-eight hours before my scheduled surgery, I suddenly experienced two strange sensations. My stomach area felt tingly and my legs felt numb. I wasn't in pain and the peculiar feeling below my waist seemed no more than annoying, in its own respect, than my sleepless nights or vanished appetite.

On the day of my surgery, I mentioned the tingling to my doctor, he suggested that it sounded like a pinched nerve that could be helped with 'wet heat,' and suggested that I try sitting in a jacuzzi.

When the operation was completed I was confined to hobbling on bandaged feet for several weeks and coping with bandaged toes for several more. Once all the bandages were off and the swelling was reduced I noticed that I still had trouble walking. Something was definitely wrong, not with my toes, but with my legs.

Two weeks before the Olympics began I hosted a party at my home for the British Olympic Association Supporters. A team doctor was present and when a friend told him of her concern for my legs, he took me aside and exacted a promise that I would make an appointment with a neurosurgeon immediately.

'But I'm not in pain,' I explained.

'I know,' he replied, 'But numbness can be more dangerous than pain.'

Following his advice, I managed to see a neurosurgeon within forty-eight hours of my party. I was ushered in to see a very young, darkly-tanned man, wearing a doctor's smock, and sporting a gold earring in his left earlobe. I was given a fifteen-minute cursory examination, in which, among other things, I was asked to walk across the room on the balls of my feet, distinguish (without looking) which toes were being pin-pricked by the doctor, and hold my balance by bending from side to side. Once back in the doctor's office, I was told that my condition 'looked like nerve damage, a viral infection or multiple sclerosis.' I was advised that there was a complete battery of expensive, painful, but in-conclusive MS tests that could be made available to me, but he advised against putting myself through that ordeal because the results were so inconclusive. Instead, he suggested I get my affairs in order, and notify him of any further 'neurological relapses'. He then walked me to the door, placed his hand on my shoulder and said, 'Good Luck'.

In a half hour, my whole life had been turned upside down. Whatever lessons I'd learned in life so far, had, alas, left me ill-equipped to cope with a short-circuited neuromuscular system. As I drove back home my only thought was how to protect my sons should my condition deteriorate.

A few days later I confided my frightening news to a dear friend and an appointment was made for me to see a famous internist who was friends with the regeneratively healthy Norman Cousins. The appointment lasted most of the day while every square inch of me, it seemed, was poked and prodded and measured and calculated. The following Saturday, the internist called me at home to say he was in the office reviewing my test results. Would I please come to his office first thing Monday morning for a consultation? Although I entered his office scared out of my wits, our meeting surprised me. Every standard medical test indicated that I was a superbly healthy woman. The mystery of my wobbly legs remained unsolved and my sense of confusion increased.

Yet another friend, hearing of my 'medical mystery', begged me to see her doctor who had returned many of her friends to health. His alternative medicine tests revealed that my adrenal glands were depleted and that my body was not processing the nutrients I ate. My red blood corpuscles, which should have been round when viewed under a microscope, were shaped like tear-drops. I was given a list of dietary supplements to take, told to enroll in yoga classes, and advised that regular spinal stimulation and adjustment would help. This advice helped, but none of the three doctors had agreed with each other.

Following the neurosurgeon's advice, I attempted to continue life as usual. But horseback riding resulted in two additional jumping mishaps, which gave me a torn shoulder blade and a permanently scarred lower lip. So I reluctantly accepted that my legs were simply not strong enough to continue my love affair with horses. I mourned my loss and packed away the boots, the breeches, the saddle and the horse-show paraphernalia that had been as much a part of my life as my work-a-day wardrobe or my everyday earrings.

I faithfully attended yoga classes – as often as three times a week when time permitted – and I swallowed endless numbers of pills.

Today, almost three years after my toe surgery, my legs are slowly recovering. They are no longer numb and they tingle (a feeling as if my thigh bone is actually a switched-on fluorescent light bulb) only on rare occasions. While I can usually walk without limping, walking from one street to the next can be a challenge and still I dare not ride. Since moving to the UK I have continued to seek medical advice which – like that in America – has largely been expensive, inconclusive and confusing.

This mystery forced me to rethink my life and vocabulary. I learned to no longer 'assume' that my body would do everything I asked it to. Five years ago I asked for – and got – releves, splits and fouettes as well as stirrup-less posting trots, serial one-stride jumps, and smooth canter-trot transitions. Last year all I asked of my body was the ability to walk down the street without embarrassing my children or myself.

After over a dozen different doctors – on both sides of the Atlantic – struggled and failed to restore my 'neuromuscular functions', I finally found a Tunbridge Wells health practitioner who restored the use of my legs. And with his help I was able to come to terms with the conflicting – and often confusing – diagnoses, which ranged from nerve damage to arthritis to an allergy to the toe-surgery anaesthesia to the dreaded MS.

The woebegone saga changed my life, for I am a totally different woman than the one who discovered that she couldn't walk properly back in 1984. Wrestling with embarrassing episodes, (like falling flat on my face at work), anxiety-ridden sleepless nights, and a deep sense of social isolation (because it's easier to stay home and watch TV than risk annoying your friends or embarrassing yourself if you have to walk too far or climb stairs or whatever), has taught me a few harsh lessons about the real issues of life.

Before my health broke down I demanded a great deal of myself and expected almost as much from the people in my life. I don't do that any more. I consider walking down the street a joyous experience and everything beyond that is practically a miracle. This has freed me from fretting over material wish lists, social climbing, and the quest for the perfect wardrobe – key pre-occupations of my LA life. Knowing how easily the trappings of 'the good life' can be snatched away has taught me that what's inside of us is the only thing that really matters.

Most of the contributors to this book have enjoyed robust good health their entire lives. But a few of the special women have had an instructional brush with ill health; I suspect that it has left each of them stronger and wiser and better acquainted with their inner selves.

Although willowy Arabella Pollen hasn't had a specific medical problem, she admits that her health has been less than robust.

Yes, I think my health has affected me – nothing bad at all but I've always been very susceptible to things and they always hit me at bad times. I have had to take time off work when I could least spare it. I had pneumonia last winter, followed by a post viral syndrome, which is something that can stay for years. You cannot get rid of it and nobody knew what it was so for five months I was just out. I was crying every day and I had this mysterious thing and nobody knew what it was; I really thought I was going batty. I thought it was the shrink for me and then I found somebody (my cousin, who's a cardiologist) who said 'This is what you have got and it's nothing to be worried about. It will go, you have just got to fight it.'

When I was at school I had the same leg problem that George Best had. It's a hereditary knee disease and my brother had it as well. That meant that I had to have both my legs in plaster for six months. I was fourteen so it hit me at a bad teenage time. I was back in England after having lived in New York, I was in between schools, and I was miserable because I am very sporty.

The only thing that kept me going at boarding school was being able to play sport, yet there I was immobilized for six months and in a great deal of pain. Trying to recover afterwards meant that the whole thing took a big chunk out of my life. I had always been a gymnast and the illness just wiped everything out completely, so I know what it's like to have your body exert its own will.

Pat Booth looks like a true picture of health, but she is another woman who has learned not to take good health for granted. Although she hasn't suffered a traumatic health reversal, her body's weak link demands that she keep a constant watch over her diet and stamina.

When I'm pregnant I get diabetes. I have a tendency to diabetes so I have to be careful and that means I'm constantly on a diet. I have to be very careful about getting too tired – it's part of the diabetes syndrome, so I have to be watchful of that. Come eight o'clock each night, I'm absolutely wiped out, so I do tend to go to bed very early. I am very cautious of over-doing it or eating the wrong foods.

Emma Nicolson, who seems capable of handling any problem life might throw her way, told me that she has a special empathy for those affected by health problems. She admitted that her life had been affected by her body's shortcomings in more ways than one.

I've mainly been affected by my hearing because I'm quite deaf. In addition to that problem, I had a very bad concussion about fifteen years ago; I fell off a motor bike in France and was knocked out and was ill for a long time after that. It taught me patience because I had to hang on in there for a long time to get back to normal. It taught me again that it doesn't really matter where you are in life, what matters is what you do with a particular situation you are faced with – rather like making the most of where you are born. It doesn't matter where you are born, it matters what you do about it.

When I lay there, knocked out and unconscious, I found it very difficult because I had to learn to speak again and my left side was paralysed. I was very poorly for a long time. It taught

154

me, profoundly, that you can't choose the pack of cards you are dealt at any given moment, but what you can choose is what you do with them. And it doesn't really matter whether you are brilliant and fully capable physically or whether you're not. What matters is how you deal with the situation that you have been given to deal with. That situation, sometimes in life, simply isn't yours to choose but what counts is how you cope with the tiny little circumscribed confine you find yourself in, with the limited abilities at your command. It took me about two years to regain my health, but I learned more from that experience than anything else.

Lady Porter looks like she's never had so much as a head cold, but her health has been the source of a few surprises over the years. She told me that, in both of the instances where she'd faced medical surprises, that she emerged stronger – mentally and physically.

Twenty-five years ago, when I was on a ski trip, I broke my leg very badly and I finished up in the local hospital. That was quite an experience for me because I had never had much sympathy for disabled people, and I think you learn by your experiences. In fact, that's the number one lesson, learn by your experience, don't just lie there thinking, 'Oh God', but 'Okay, what can I do?' Nobody there spoke any French, nobody spoke anything except German, and they were very much not of this world at all. I got myself a professor who came in to teach me German, so instead of lying there and bewailing my fate, I started to learn German. It takes quite a lot of getting over, a major break, because you've got a whole new kind of world, and you have to sort it out, not feel sorry for yourself, and learn by it. I think one of the frightening experiences in the hospital was that they had one entire floor of people who were mildly lunatic as a result of inbreeding. On the first walk that I took, a terribly exhausting walk after being in a leg plaster, I got downstairs and it was like the film *Snakepit*, with these unfortunate people all crowded round me and me trying to get out. That wasn't very nice.

Another time I actually had this experience where you are outside yourself looking in. I very nearly conked out.

When I was four, I had my tonsils out and in those days, things used to go wrong more easily. There was a little group of us having the procedure and my cousin got blood poisoning and died; I didn't but I was left with poison shreds. They scraped it later when I was fourteen but it means I now don't have any protection in my throat. I pick things up easily and twelve or fifteen years ago we went skiing and I got a throat bug; my throat closed up and they thought I had diphtheria. It completely closed and the doctor who was there was shouting at me, and my brother-in-law was there with a knife, and he was going to do a tracheotomy. He didn't know what to do, but he knew he had to do something. I was going blue. I could see it because I was out there looking at the scene; fortunately the doctor got a spoon down my throat and it opened up and they carted me off. It was ulcers in the oesophagus.

Now, I'm very into the body, how you handle your health, what you do with it, stress and looking after the body and I'm very aware of my body. I think my illnesses taught me that you have got to fight, because you can just give in and go – not with a broken leg, but if you are very ill, you can just slide away. I do exercises once a week and I have a treatment once a week of acupuncture or acupressure. I go off to health farms to get out and about and away, I even went on a self-hypnosis course; I can't do it but I use it for relaxation. I do anything that can help me keep a balance because I find I'm all head sometimes and your head can take over. I find it very difficult to switch off. The other thing that I find difficult is that I'm a very physical person but because I'm so busy, I don't get enough exercise. Yesterday I walked down twenty-five flights of stairs because I knew otherwise I wasn't going to get any exercise that day.

Lynda Chalker told me that her brush with illness changed the whole course of her life.

I had glandular fever as a student and because I was sick, I didn't finish my maths degree. Instead I got a degree in statistics and I'm a very much more practical person as a result of it. That course gave me the necessary background to have a thirteen year career in commerce before I went into the House of Commons, so thanks to glandular fever, I became much more used to industry. It wasn't fun having it, though, because it took four months before they found out what it was and then I was ill for another three or four months after that.

What all these women have learned is that we can't assume that our bodies are simply machines programmed to always do whatever we tell them to. Sometimes – as in my case – they are teachers that force us to slow down, recuperate, and start to see ourselves (and our world) from a different perspective.

6

Image

Robert Burns surely had women in mind when he reminded us that we don't see ourselves as others see us. I know that my self-image as the 1980s Mary Tyler Moore came tumbling to the ground with a thud when my children – without malice or hostility – told me they thought my image was more reminiscent of a career woman version of Ma Walton. So much for my self-image!

Often we are surprised to learn that others perceive within us strengths or weaknesses, virtues or flaws of which we are totally unaware. 'Where', we ask ourselves, 'did they get that idea about me?' The answer, of course, is that they received signals – often times subliminal ones – that provided them with information about us that we either didn't know ourselves or knew but hoped to suppress.

One of my former colleagues at the *Daily Mail*, over a very liquid Fleet Street luncheon, once told me how I reminded him of a puppy dog just hoping and waiting for attention and affection. Smiling noncommittally, I felt the torturous flush of embarrassment turn every inch of skin above my collar-bone an undesirable shade of scarlet. With an inward groan, I asked myself how it was possible for me to project a supplicatory image. My discomfort was increased, of course, by the fact that there was more than a grain of truth to my colleague's observations.

Although real maturity results in our image truthfully reflecting the 'real' person inside, it takes loads of experience to reach that state. Knowing that our image is the advertisement that proceeds the product, however, can help us ensure that we don't broadcast conflicting messages.

Shirley Conran said that her public image wasn't terribly important to her. As she explained it:

When it comes to image or looks I think there are three factors. There's you as you really are; you as you see yourself; and you as how others see you. You don't have much control over how others will see you or label you, so I think you have to put that concern out of your mind and focus instead on how you feel about your own looks.

Claire Rayner, whose motherly visage denies any hint of vanity, told me that the most important focus of her image is her *coiffeur*.

I swim every morning, and my favourite luxury is having my hairdresser fix my hair each morning as soon as my exercise is finished. I don't splurge on clothes or make-up, but I regard my hair as an essential expense.

Almost as if her late husband were still quietly urging her to upscale her wardrobe, Sally Burton told me:

Sometimes I think to myself, I have really got to smarten up – not when I am in London as I am dressed up then, but when I'm at home slopping around the garden I sometimes think, 'God, this is not on, this is not right. I should be smartened up.' Many people at the exercise class say, 'Oh yes, I know Sally. She's the one who comes along in the tracksuit and you wouldn't know who she was.'

Sometimes I feel that it is expected of me to dress up and at times I really enjoy it. I love clothes. I hate fashion and I tend to buy very classic clothes that are well made out of beautiful fabrics that last a long time.

Jane Packer spoke in terms of her body and her image as a woman. Like so many of us, she wishes she were thinner.

I don't think anybody is ever really happy with the way they look and I'm certainly not. Sometimes I just feel trapped within the wrong body. I really should be at least ten inches taller, I should be thinner, and everybody wants to look different. On one of those days when you are feeling confident and you are chatting away to somebody and suddenly you catch sight of yourself in the mirror with surprise.

I'm a great people-watcher, I love to watch people and you look at so many people and think, 'Oh she looks lovely,' or 'that's really nice about her, how come I haven't got that?' I think my major hang-up is my legs. I would just love to have longer legs. I'm only about five feet four inches. I'm always looking at those girls in short skirts. I could diet forever but my legs are never going to get any longer and my knees are never going to get thinner.

Pat Booth, who still retains the good looks of a professional model, told me that she is aware of her distinctive style. But the problem is, she doesn't like it!

I see myself as a six foot brunette when I'm really a five foot six inch blonde. When I catch a passing glimpse of myself I am surprised at what I see. My image of myself is not how I am visually but I still play up my visual self because I know it works; I will use it almost like a cliché. After all, I have a kind of cliché look; I walk in the door and people say, 'Oh yes, there's a blue-eyed blonde.' It's a very identifiable look and I play on that a great deal and use it often in business, especially where men are concerned. I use it because I think if you have been given an asset you might as well use it. Having said that, I don't particularly like my visual appearance. I'd like to look like Paloma Picasso, for example, I like that kind of look; I think it's so elegant. When I get a look at myself, I'm always in a rush so I've got hair flying, pieces of fabric coming off me and flying in the breeze and so on. Not at all what you'd call elegant.

Lady Porter told me that she had enrolled in the 'Colour Me Beautiful' programme to simplify her wardrobe. Other than that technique, which she said helped to 'streamline and speed things up', she seems to lean towards a carefree and uncluttered approach to her looks. Lady Porter said:

When I was a kid I used to think I was very ugly and that worried me enormously. Now it doesn't worry me particularly. My public image seems to me to vary. I'm surprised at how people see me. I think I'm a nice, quiet, easy-going creature and they think I'm a dragon lady. I think that's my public image, or possibly just somebody who gets things done. I'm a very informal person. I'm very direct, I don't bother to dress it up, I say what I think.

Tall women can be excused for weighing more than their shorter sisters. But Celia Brayfield, who is far from petite, is quite happy to talk about her size, as she explains.

I'm five feet ten and about 160 to 170 pounds and my weight varies quite a bit, but I'm a big woman. It means that you can look a man of six foot five just about in the eye. I've also got a strong face – bone structure. It's the best thing – I don't know how women of five feet two live – being tall means that you can talk to a man and he hears you. I remember once – you know the journalist called Molly Parkin, she's a little Welsh woman – she's pretty bizarre and she was quite pissed at a party and was saying, 'You are a really tall, wonderful woman. You are an Amazon, why don't you stand up straight?' and the answer was that I was bending down to listen to her. I couldn't stand up straight and hear her because she was so short and I was so tall – it's quite an impediment with communication.

Arabella Pollen's career is devoted to helping women look good. But when it comes to her own public image, she is beset with the same insecurities as the rest of us.

I don't like my public image very much. I don't think I have a public image, but having said that people here are very willing to put you into a category and I think I have that played on me a great deal because of my background. People assume that I've made it because I've been given loads of money by my parents – but that isn't true – not at all. But in the fashion world, unless you have an East End accent and come from a slum, people can be very suspicious of you. It's a reverse class discrimination. I'm from a perfectly good middle-class family, but they think that I made it because I was given money by my parents simply because they happened to have a house in the country. It just doesn't work like that. Some people are too ignorant – or just don't care to find out – so they brand you and once you are branded, it's very difficult to get rid of that image. It annoys me terrifically because I think it comes from ignorance and stupidity and it really bugs me.

When it comes to clothes, I wear my own designs because I can't afford anybody else. I always do. I think everyone is really unhappy with something about the way they look. On the whole I think I'm lucky, I've got two arms and two legs, but sure I hate my legs, and other things about the way I look, just the same as any female.

Prue Leith spent her adolescence feeling clumsy. Now she is a tall, strikingly attractive woman, but the memory of being too big and gawky remains with her, decades later.

I think on a personal level the only thing I feel that I have overcome is that when I was young I hated being so tall, so big and, I thought, so fat. If I see photographs now of me when I was sixteen, I think I looked wonderful, but at the time, I thought I was huge. I'm five feet eight and a half inches tall – it seemed bigger then – not so much big but clumsy. I can remember what my mother said once – and I held this deeply against her and she laughs about it now and I laugh too – when I had some young boyfriend I was trying to impress, and I brought a tea tray into the room and, of course, put it down crooked and knocked all the cups over in my usual clumsy manner. My mother, in exasperation, which I can quite understand, said, 'Oh my God, it is just like having a horse in the house,' and that's exactly what I felt like; a lot of my adolescence and early university days, I felt like a horse knocking things down.

I could be trusted to tread on people and I was the one who would step backwards in the aisle, which I did in Johannesburg on the first night of a play. I actually knocked the Mayor of Johannesburg down because he was only a little fellow and I stepped back far too quickly. Or sometimes I would be talking and I would swing round and hit something. I gradually learned to control my movements a bit, but I have also learned to realize that it isn't important, there are lots of clumsy people about.

The thing that I don't like about my appearance is that I think I look like a Mother's Pride flour advertisement – very homely and reassuring and all that. Actually, I want to be terribly glamorous and chic and also I wish I wasn't so huge – I wish to be nine and a half stone instead of eleven stone – wouldn't we all?

In the PR field, Lynne Franks has had the public image of a nonconformist for well over a decade. She told me:

When I first started my business, in 1970, I was dressed very bizarrely; I had bright orange hair, bowler hats and mad jewellery but that was the fashion in those days and I have always loved fashion, so that was right, but I used to have millions of people who thought I was very bizarre. The clients that I have now – in a large international company – they loved

162

me and they always thought I was great. They thought I was completely potty – I would walk in with black nail polish and they would pat me on the head and say, 'What is she wearing today?' but because I was good at my job and because, I hope, they respected me it didn't matter. I now choose to dress in a different way and if I want to play certain roles when I'm wearing a nice suit it's okay, but I never compromise myself to become what I am not. At times I ought to, sometimes I should keep my mouth shut and I should learn to keep my mouth shut much more than I do, but if I think something is wrong I will say so. I will not back down.

Audrey Slaughter seemed less confident about her image, but in a cheerfully resigned way accepts that it's quasi-normal to not be pleased with one's looks.

I don't know what my public image is except that it is consistent. People are quite surprised when they meet me that I am fairly normal, but I don't like my looks. I hate my hair, which is faded now of course. It was a flaming red and I was always trying to dye it but it was such a strong colour the dyes just made it look as if I hadn't washed my hair. I had my teeth straightened and I am fat now whereas I used to be thin and more curvaceous; now I am too curvaceous. Do you know anyone who is pleased with the way they look?

I think people do think I am a tough go-getter Fleet Street lady, but I am not a Fleet Street lady in that manner. I do think people assume that of journalists generally.

Elizabeth Emanuel told me:

In my business it's quite difficult because you have got to look like a designer. You feel you are expected to look brilliantly dressed, which I find a problem because usually we do interviews and things at the last minute. For me it's usually a real hassle to get the make-up on. I try and look nice and I'm very conscious that I've got to make an effort because when I haven't, and I see the results later, it's really upsetting. So it's quite important to try to be together. Of course, I would like to try to lose a lot of weight.

Non-verbal messages

I don't know what my non-verbal messages are, but I am aware of sending signals that don't help me get what I want. The first part of my dual-barrelled delivery may be the result of a semi-permanent pucker between my eyebrows; it has been referred to, in unflattering instances, as a constant worry frown. This prompts people to think I'm upset or angry even when I'm not.

The bigger problem, for me, is that I have been unable to express what is important to me without getting *aggressive* about the situation. Perhaps because I am hyper-aware of other people's feelings, I am continually baffled at people's inability to perceive what is bothering me. As I've lamented to my children and close friends on more than one occasion, 'Why can't I get the message across without starting World War Three?'

So my task for the coming year is to find a way to either surround myself with more sensitive, aware individuals or else take a communication course that will teach me how to get the message across – at home, at the office and in my personal life.

The messages we unconsciously transmit *do* affect our effectiveness as women. What others assume about us – and what we're trying to convey – can add untold grey hairs and those unwelcome facial expressions that signal 'out of control'.

Ruby Wax told me that she was baffled by the way other people perceived her.

> I read things saying I'm loud on the 'Don't Miss Wax' show, but I don't know where that comes from. I'm sure I'm not talking loud, but maybe that's how I am when I get nervous. To others I'm being outrageous or stuff, but to me I'm just asking normal questions.

And Elizabeth Emanuel said her height conveys a mesage that can be totally misleading. 'A lot of people think I'm a soft touch, probably because of being small. But I'm not.'

Prue Leith said she was bemused by her 'dragon lady' persona, which bothers her.

> I know that I am scary to my employees – not all of them and not the senior ones (the senior ones know very well that they can shout back) – but the junior ones; but that may be just because

of my elevated rank. You don't see the boss very often because they're in subsidiary companies and I only turn up once every term to do demonstrations. So all the teachers think 'Oh God, she will say the pans are dirty, etc.,' and because I am tactless I do tend to say first, 'The coffee pans need cleaning,' then I'll comment 'Oh, aren't the flowers pretty.' My husband is exactly the same. I'm always saying 'Just tell me the nice things first then I'll be able to stand the criticism,' I can't do that but I keep telling my husband he ought to do it.

We have a girl who runs our cookery school who is a dear friend and I adore her and she will say to me 'Can you be very gentle with so and so' (one of her staff members or teachers) or 'By the way, I have given you so and so for a demonstration assistant, so please be kind to her because she is very young or she is terrified of you.' I get very annoyed and say '*Why* is she terrified of me?'

I find it very hurtful. I feel very hurt that I have got this image. I was terrified of my mother though, because I thought she was a powerful woman. I must be like that. I was talking to my daughter about it and she said 'Well, you are frightening, mum. Terrifying,' and I find that very sad because I always try to be nice.

Audrey Slaughter has had her own perception problems at work. In her words:

I think I give the impression of being vague to some people because I am thinking of other things and I don't always seem to notice. I do notice but I don't know what to comment on something until afterwards. Also, I think I am very bad sometimes at not giving praise where praise is due. It seems as if I'm indifferent in that I expect them to do good work, so when they turn in good work I just accept it. I don't say 'Oh, that's a marvellous piece', whereas if they did something very good or exceptionally interesting I would then say 'That was a very good piece', meaning it was excellent.

Now that I'm writing for other people as a freelancer, I very much appreciate one editor on *The Daily Telegraph* who always says something nice when I have spent hours on a piece and hand it in. I didn't realize then how people felt about their work. I worked in a rarefied atmosphere and one or two of my ex-staff have worked out a wonderful cabaret; they did one sketch when a new girl started and I was going along the corridor and when I saw her I thought she was another girl who was leaving and I said 'Are you still here?' and the poor girl had only been employed six weeks and she scuttled back to the office obviously thinking 'I'm going to get sacked.'

Occasionally people say to me 'Oh, you are so normal, I have always been afraid of you.' People who have heard of me and don't know me say this and then I wonder 'What messages am I conveying?' and 'What do people think of me?'

Sally Burton, who didn't seem at all distant when I met her, told me:

I take my time to get to know people and that sometimes means I am described as stand-offish. It is just that I stand back a bit. I think I have to be a little aware of who I am and people seeking me out. I am aware that there is an element of celebrity and I think I get quite sensitive about how I am received. Well, I suppose it goes back to criticism . . . I think generally I am received quite well. I am surprised when people say 'But you are so nice.' Well, what did they think I was going to be? I think maybe people think I might have changed because of the glittery life.

Arabella Pollen, whom I would never describe as 'aggressive', surprised me when she spoke of her imagined non-verbal messages.

I think I probably look quite aggressive not that I dress that way. I'm not really aware of conveying anything. I never really know what people think of me unless they actually tell me. I know that I am quite aggressive in business, so probably I feel that I think people can see that. I don't like being very aggressive, but I am because you have to be to survive – but, obviously I don't like to be portrayed as an aggressive woman.

Emma Nicolson also spoke of being perceived in a way that wasn't flattering:

I'm sure that people sometimes think I ignore them, but that's because if they speak behind me perhaps I don't hear them. There's nothing I can do about that, but that's a reality. It's a nuisance. Apart from that I don't know how people see me – I haven't asked them.

Lady Porter knows that she can't hide her thoughts.

I've got a very expressive face. And I know that sometimes too much comes through. I try and control it, but if I'm impatient I'll show it and obviously body language counts for a lot. If I'm doing things, it can show through; it's a drawback.

Brenda Dean feels that people have branded her with an unwanted Mrs Thatcher look-alike image. Laughingly she told me:

I know that people feel I look like the Prime Minister and a number of people say that. I think it's the skin and hair colour and the length of the hair. I'm aware of that and I understand; my eyesight has started to go so at a distance I can't make out people's features so if someone 'looks' like someone else, I do understand. But I didn't ten years ago. People sometimes say: 'You look like a younger version of Mrs Thatcher.' Sometimes they're not as polite as that.

I know that sometimes my appearance may be stiffly groomed, wearing nail varnish and nice clothes and jewellery is not the image that trade unions have so sometimes I come across as a bit stiff. I can't change, I'm comfortable as I am. People think that because you are in the trade union movement, that shabby is okay, but people who think that don't know the people I represent. I can remember when I was Branch Secretary, they provided you with a car up to a certain sum. There were only three of us there and they didn't specify which car you had to have so I chose an MGB sports car. I was the first Trade Union officer I think (certainly in our union) to turn up in a sports car. When I first got it, I thought: 'Oh God, what are the men going to think about this?' For a while it was off the road and the branch had a little mini van so I borrowed that while my car was being fixed. One of the FOCs took me aside and said: 'Brenda, you're not going to keep the van are you, because we think it's great when the management sees you turn up in a sports car.' And it's the same with clothes. I won't look scruffy because the women I represent take a pride in their appearance and the men like someone looking nice around them. I feel uncomfortable if there's a scruffy bloke sitting next to me. It does affect the way you work. I wouldn't have anyone working for me who was scruffy.

Pat Booth has a seductive public image even though she prefers to be with women instead of men.

I think because of the way I look I project sexual messages or sensual ones. I think my image is quite a sexy one – when I'm scrubbed up, that is. I think that this can cause problems – I usually know when men react that way and then I have to play to the women of the room rather than the men because I am afraid of alienating the women. I'm much more relaxed with women. I like them much more than men. In a way, I still somehow see men as a threat – I don't know how to handle them, I don't know who they are, I don't know where they're coming from. I know part of the time what they want because it's so obvious and animalistic it's ridiculous, and so I back off from that and I find my close relationships are always women. I'm much happier with them.

Jane Packer, who works incredibly hard, admits to feeling confused about the non-verbal messages her lifestyle demands.

I feel at the moment that I am living two lives because since my profile appeared in *Options Magazine*, I have been doing lots of press on the shop, interviews and things like that and I just think 'Well, here I am, I am doing these things and people out there are listening to me do my little bit.' Then I have to get back to work, roll up the sleeves, get soil under the fingernails and be up at four o'clock in the morning and work until ten at night. Sometimes I feel like asking 'Where am I?' I'm pretending to be this successful person but what is a successful person? The two lifestyles are not compatible, they haven't met in the middle and they hopefully will, because I just can't keep this up for much longer.

Arabella Pollen seemed to know intuitively that we give many different non-verbal messages – both intentionally and accidentally. In her words:

You have to be a chameleon if you are female. I think you have to have lots of disguises and you have to have lots of different aspects to your personality. People respond to you in different ways and there are times when I meet people when I have to put on my professional, high-heeled city suit, professional attitude. I don't like to convey just one particular image; you just have to do what you feel.

Self-imposed limitations

Who among us doesn't do something that impedes our forward progress? I, for one, know that my biggest self-saboteur is impatience, and it has cost me plenty.

Perhaps one of the reasons I find the company of old people so comforting is that they rarely (unlike me) fly into a panic at the first hint of trouble. Age somehow teaches them that everything will eventually evolve for the best – even if things don't immediately seem to work out the way they might have wished. Surely it is immature ego that has prompted me to feel that I have to *force* events to follow the scenario in my mind. After doing so, on several occasions, I've been left with a bad case of exhaustion, a sense that what I so desperately wanted wasn't really in my best interest, and the normal fall-out that accompanies any pyrrhic victory.

When I interviewed the twenty women who agreed to be part of this project I learned that many of them were also aware of some trait or chosen lifestyle that hobbled them.

I found Brenda Dean's discussion of how she'd limited her growth – in a non-professional way – poignant, even though she smiled throughout the entire conversation.

The self-imposed limitation I have put on myself is not having children but that wasn't because I sat down one day and said, 'I'm not going to do that and that and that.' I was just enjoying my job so much (and I still am); but when I think about it, the real reason was that I didn't want to be tied down.

Thank God, it's no longer like the last generation where if you were a single parent you didn't have a choice – if I'd had a child I would never have got the job of General Secretary, I would have been branded a loose woman. I couldn't have left this job, had a child, and come back – so in that way childlessness was self imposed. I say to the bright women in our union, 'Don't do what I did, if you want a child, you go and do it. The Union dare not stop you.' We have had three women officers in the last few years who have had children; one of them, on our Executive Council, was pregnant and we wondered how the men were going to react, but no one said a word.

Elizabeth Emanuel admits that she is not as indiscriminately friendly as she might be. In her words:

I know with my character I can cause problems by being difficult with certain types of people; I say 'I either like them or I don't', then I am really awful to be with. My husband, David, is very good with *everybody* and will just talk to everybody, whereas I find it more difficult because I'm not that sort of person.

Detta O'Cathain's simultaneous need for stimulation and routine strikes her as a potential problem.

I really think that I am one of these people who finds it difficult to concentrate without continual stimulus; in a continual repetitious environment I get very bored. On the other hand I have to say that I quite like routine, I like some areas of routine that are, by their very nature, repetitive. But generally speaking with people, I like people to be fresh, I like new ideas, meeting new people, new circumstances.

Ruby Wax told me that she had limited her growth by buying into her family's belief that she was dumb.

I got my success at thirty-four, I find that a little peculiar. I couldn't even write until I was thirty because my father told me I was dumb so you know that button in your head. Until I got some very helpful therapy I couldn't tap the ability to write because the panic set in; it would just shut on and off. In my brain I would remind myself that I got Cs in English. I couldn't tap it but it would come up by accident, it was weird, a weird thing because you would freak out thinking 'this is a fluke'. Now I just sit down and it goes, so that's why now I think I am a writer.

Emma Nicolson told me that she sees physical exercise as her self-imposed limitation.

I would like to be fitter but I don't always take the trouble to go swimming even though I like being fitter, but for some reason I have a mental handicap that I won't get fitter.

Novelist Pat Booth's limitations are, she feels, not so much physical as emotional.

I put tremendous emotional limitations on myself. I would not, for example, ever be in a situation where I would have an affair outside my marriage because I impose those limitations. I don't believe people fall in love with somebody and have an affair – they're looking for an affair and then they find one. That's not to do with the fact that I'm moral, it's to do with the fact that I couldn't handle it. It would just crumble my life and my organized day-to-day existence would crash. I'd fall apart and fall in passion; I keep myself very much in check.

Two limitations affected Lady Porter's life. One was the decision to put family first and the second was her limited scholastic accomplishments. She told me:

My self-imposed limitation was that I decided to keep my family number one. I think that's self imposed because I was asked to go into Parliament ten years ago and I thought about it and I decided that I wasn't prepared to give everything else up. I like to have a bit of spectrum. I don't want to be tunnelled. My lack of schooling wasn't self imposed. It was imposed upon me. Once again for really rather strange reasons.

Because I was very young, as a prefect and due to the war, it was a very young scene and the school's headmistress would select the girls who were going to stand to be head and then the school would vote on them. She seemed to be reluctant to put me forward. I was the top prefect and they knew that I would get it because all the junior school would vote for me. I've always been the sort of person you either hate or love, and what happened in the end was that it got to a stage where it looked pretty obvious that she didn't want to have 'Cohen' on the notice board, so I left at fifteen after taking what was then the School Certificate. (I was somebody who never did their homework, I used to be very good at history and English and all that. I was terrible at maths; I hated it and I hated the teachers.)

Prue Leith feels she limits herself for her husband's sake.

I definitely do less than I would normally because I don't want to worry Rayne. My husband thinks I do too much as it is and he is very much more cautious than me and so I do tend to cut back, though he would be surprised to hear it because he still thinks I do too much. He doesn't know how much I turn down, don't do or dinners I don't go to.

I do swallow hard and say no to a lot of things, books, programmes, etc., because I know it will put too much of a strain on my family.

Audrey Slaughter, who is viewed as a real dynamo by many people in publishing told me that her shyness has kept her from doing lots of things.

I am basically very, very shy and when there's a party with celebrities there, I can't bring myself to 'rubberneck' round them because I think they think everybody's after them. So I miss talking to lots of people because I think, 'Oh they won't want to come and talk to me', it's ridiculous, particularly in a journalist, whereas my husband Charles would go charging up and start talking, but I am afraid to.

Rock bottom

I don't know about you, but when I hit rock bottom (emotionally) I cry. Since I am not a woman normally given to tears, crying signifies that I am well on my way to becoming unhinged.

The closest I've ever been to a total state of despair came two years ago when my younger son chose to return to America and live with his father. My emotions were already stretched to the breaking point by financial problems, the pressures of working on Fleet Street, terminal loneliness, and my enforced immobility due to the mysterious problem with my legs. I couldn't find a single thing to be optimistic or happy about and, between sniffles, I confided to a California friend that my whole life was in shambles.

'The woman who rarely weeps' became 'she who always has tears in her eyes'. I even missed a full day off work at the *Daily Mail* because I couldn't stop crying – a first for me. For close to two months I wallowed in this mire of depression, telling myself that no one really needed me and, because of my health problem, I was an unwelcome burden to both my family and my friends.

This pathetic chapter in my life could have continued indefinitely had I not had the opportunity to return home to LA for a long overdue two-week visit. The cloud that had hung over my head was slowly diluted by dear friends who – either due to or in spite of my year-long absence – saw me through eyes filled with envy, admiration and pride. Whereas I had viewed my life as a never-ending chronicle of rejection, disappointment and hurt, the friends I'd left behind made no secret that they saw me as an accomplished, independent woman with an enviable career in one of the world's most desirable cities.

By the time my 747 touched down at Heathrow, my wounded ego was once again in serviceable order. I was able to return to my flat and sit in my son's empty bedroom without bursting into tears. My friendship support system had taught me, in the nicest possible way, that what I had viewed as the end of the world was merely the end – the natural and even healthy end – of one of my life's chapters.

Shirley Conran told me her formula for coping with life's challenges – she relies on her children!

> When the chips are down, I turn to my sons. I go to Jasper if I need guidance or reassurance for emotional or moral issues and I turn to Sebastian if there's a practical problem that I can't solve. They are my strength and they've been marvellous sons.

Lynne Franks returns to Buddhism when life hardly seems worth living, while Elizabeth Emanuel gave me her (highly identifiable) formula for beating the blues: '. . . my friends, my family, television and food, in that order.'

Emma Nicolson didn't look for strength when she was in her darkest moment because she was busy trying to give solace to others. She recalled:

> When I was caught up in the Brighton bombing, which I suppose would be the sort of darkest hour you are referring to, when we were all blown up at the Conservative Party conference four years ago, I didn't turn to anybody at all. My job was to help other people.

Ruby Wax hibernates when life becomes depressing. In her words, 'I travel; I go off on my own. I go to major hotels and check into a room – back to the womb, for three whole days sometimes. I just don't come out.'

But Celia Brayfield told me that she has to *do* something whenever she feels really low.

I'm very wary of what's called the comfort of religion. I think a lot of what is called the comfort of religion is not a lot better than chanting, simply it's often something familiar that permits you to switch off your mind.

I do find, however, that religious ritual and the Bible can be comforting; I'm not flourishing and I'm not wicked, but I can only go so far with that. When the chips are down and I'm waking up at three o'clock in the morning with my hair standing on end, the only thing that actually does any good is taking action. You can have the self-knowledge to know what is really going on (which is not always exactly what you think it is), but actually that's the only thing I do.

Sally Burton has a close male friend who can put a smile on her face no matter how sad she feels.

I have one particular friend – a male friend – whom I turn to. He has been so good to me over the past three years. I can phone at any time day or night and he will cancel commitments to come and stay with me; I am immensely grateful for that. He remembers everything – even my wedding anniversary. I am not going to marry him – he is just a wonderful friend and I am so fortunate. Also, what is so great is that he is a man because at the end of a relationship, you miss male conversation. You know when you are just feeling terrible, he will come and take me out. He's just fantastic. And other than that, I would turn to drink!

The first thing I would do if I was feeling really desperate would be to get on the phone and call my friend, and when he had cheered me up, then I would have a drink.

Sometimes I stay in bed and I cocoon myself. It is almost as if I'm afraid that by going out, someone might bump into me.

Prue Leith turns to her husband when she's feeling down.

My strength is my husband, no question – it's a boring answer but I turn to Rayne. We've been married twelve and a half years. If I'm really unhappy I have to have him around. If I'm really worried, I need his support and he is very philosophical. He's much more cautious than me but he has no regrets, so he will always make me see things in perspective. If I ever get in a state – money, manager not happy, children not doing well at school – I tend to over react. He is very good at making me see things properly, but then there's another side to inner strength, which is just being in the country. I find that if I just have time, or can ride my horse for two hours and weed a patch of garden – it's wonderful. We have a home in Oxfordshire. Recently I had a hysterectomy and I had six weeks off. At the beginning I just crept around pruning roses, but after a while I read, did a patchwork quilt, weeded great tracks of garden, and it was wonderfully peaceful; I didn't do any work that was really good. When I'm down, I want to be at home, on my own – I think I have to be alone for this.

Novelist Pat Booth has two forms of refuge when life is rocky – her husband and her religion. In her words:

My religion is a day-to-day inner strength. I turn to that even when I don't 'need' the inner strength. For example, I go to church every day, so I pray for guidance much more. When I've lost the plot in a book I do tend to turn to my husband. I find questions asked in church immediately become very clear to me – the answer becomes very, very clear and that's actually why I use my religion on a day-to-day basis. It's almost part of the structure of my day, it works. I withdraw when something major happens to me. When my mother died, for example, I just became numb and speechless. Funnily enough, I don't use religion at those times. I turn to it at a later moment, but I think it's healthy for you to experience that numbness and deadness because I think it would be tragic if we tried to avoid those heartaches. I'm very fortunate that not too many dreadful things have happened to me – only the loss of my parents. But in those moments I withdraw. But luckily, since I've been married, I don't experience it so much anymore.

I do get major depressions and I do withdraw. I call it my 'housecoat weather' and I put on a housecoat and I just don't go out. I think actually, funnily enough, part of the success of marriage is that it doesn't allow you to withdraw. There's always somebody in the house so you can't actually withdraw and I think that's probably been one of the successes of my marriage really.

I really turn to my husband but also, when there's nowhere to run to, you end up facing the problem and dealing with it rather than running.

Audrey Slaughter has her own way of dealing with depression.

I think I paint – oil paint – which gives me a different sense because I care about it, trying to get a blue light or something.
   I also talk over my problem with Charles; just talk it out. I think painting helps then sometimes I will have a drink – a large whisky and another and suddenly I find myself slightly sloshed. That's just a weakness – if I was miserable and alone I would drink and probably turn into an alcoholic. In moments of stress I do have a large scotch.

Lady Porter goes into action when she's down. Her explanation of 'down time activities' made me feel positively slothful!

I join a health club in order to get nature and music. I go right away, I want complete space but I don't need too much time. I regenerate in four or five days and I do that if I can at regular intervals; the other thing I like to do is to go scuba diving, snorkelling. I snorkel and I look at fish – I go into another world and get completely away from my problems.

Arabella Pollen quite happily told me of the source of her inner strength.

I really turn to my family. I rely very much on my brother and very much on my husband. I have four very important men in my life: my husband, my brother, my father and my son. I see all of them a lot – they're my boys. My family is my inner strength.

Saying goodbye to a victim lifestyle

Until I moved to London I ran a grave risk of becoming a professional victim. It was altogether too easy for me to adopt a 'poor me' stance whenever I didn't get my own way, faced a road-block, or felt predisposed to envy someone else's good fortune.
   It's particularly easy for women, I think, to see themselves as victims of an unjust or unfeeling world. And the more power we imagine others have – instead of acknowledging and seeking power

for ourselves – the easier it is to feel outnumbered and over-whelmed by omnipotent forces.

The problem with being a victim is that it drags you – and your expectations of yourself and life – into a slow-moving downward spiral. By convincing yourself that you are not in any way accountable for what has happened (or will happen) to you, you escape responsibility, but live in fear of the unknown *it*, which will thwart whatever dreams you may be so bold as to have. The *it* can take many forms: men, bosses, your health, your family, the government, fate, religion . . . the list of possibilities is endless.

The turning point came for me when someone told me about the initials CPA. I thought they were talking about the American acronym for Certified Public Accountant, but I later learned that they meant the role we each play in our life history. CPA stands for Create, Promote, or Allow. And if we ask ourselves if we have CPAed any event in our life we are surely able to pinpoint a case or two of culpability.

I know I played a role in creating my medical problems, for example, by neglecting my diet and sleep at a time when both could have helped preserve my health. The CPA episodes involved in the break up of my marriages would probably fill another volume.

Eliminating 'victimization' from your life means that you are forced to behave like an adult on an emotional – as well as physical – level. Once you banish the dreaded *it* from your life, you just may find, as I did, that there's a lot fewer times when the unexpected and unwelcome appear in your life. Oddly enough, by choosing not to *feel* like a victim you can reduce the number of times when events might push you in that direction.

Audrey Slaughter told me:

> I felt like a victim when I was at the *Independant*. I was there as a journalist rather than an editor; a new features editor came who had worked on magazines before, was very vague and never told anybody what he wanted. He gradually eased out three of the senior journalists and we functioned on a small staff until we appointed other people. I was fired, and at first I was very angry about it; not angry, upset. I think the editor supported me; and at first I said, 'I don't want you to say I was fired because at my stage of life it's difficult.' So I just went. In the end it didn't

matter very much. I don't have to earn a vast salary to live anymore. The children are gone, Charles is virtually retired. In fact, it's not worked out badly – I've had lots of people asking me to write for them. But at the time it was unpleasant.

Lady Porter told me that she felt like a victim when she was a young girl but the hurt she experienced then propels her, even now, to continue achieving.

Yes, I felt like a victim at school and I changed the situation by leaving. But any time I have felt a victim – I then think, 'Oh sod you, I'll show you.' I've always been somebody who, if you reject me, I say 'Sod you and I'll show you' and that gives me joy. I'm still showing them at school; I think rejection is good.

Pat Booth told me of her self-protective ability to prevent being a victim.

The moment I feel victimized I attack. I become quite aggressive. Say, for example, I found myself in a situation where a man had not called at a time he said he was going to call, I would immediately back off from that relationship, so the moment I felt victimized – even for the first time – I wouldn't allow it to go further than once.

Work situations bring out the victim feelings in Jane Packer, as she told me about her frustrations with people within her industry.

I feel more like a victim with people than in financial situations. I feel like a victim if somebody does something that upsets me; things at work more than anything else. If somebody is particularly nasty about what we do (people within the same business) – that kind of thing really upsets me. When things like that happen to me, I get very angry and the next week I will create something bigger and better – it's that kind of motivation.

Arabella Pollen told me that she is no stranger to the unwelcome sense of being a victim. In her words:

I have felt like a victim on several occasions; I haven't been able to do very much to change that.
    I have had several bad experiences with my career, things when people have taken downright advantage and I have paid for that. There was nothing I could do about it and I have been a

victim because I was stupid or whatever. But all the same, I have been in a non-blame situation, and there is very little you can do about that, you just have to fight with your self-respect and say you're going to rise above it. 'I'm not going to let it get me down.' I still plot revenge on various people who've hurt me, but it will come back to them without my help. If you are a victim, there is nothing you can do except fight back with yourself.

Emma Nicolson told me that she has learned to drastically alter her circumstances whenever she feels like a victim.

I felt very trapped when I was eighteen in a social world that didn't suit me – eighteen, nineteen, twenty – very trapped and so I broke out into something that took me right away from that. I changed my situation 100 per cent and that's what I do. If I don't like something, I'll swap the whole thing.

Designer Elizabeth Emanuel protects herself from being a victim by avoiding people who might overpower her. She says:

If there are strong people around me with very strong opinions I find it can easily sway me and in that way I become a victim because I may be persuaded to do something I may not want to do. I try to avoid being a victim by not having those people around.

Most of these women have coped with being a victim in an intelligent way. By reorganizing their emotions and pin-pointing the *source* of those feelings, they were then able to proceed to the crucial step of finding a way to prevent becoming a victim in the future.

The key here is our ability to *learn* from our life experiences. There arc endless numbers of ways in which we can become victims, but there are an equal number of solutions to help us avoid victim-scenario repeat performances.

Falling into the habit of being the 'poor victim' is easy, and taking charge of your own life can be a challenging assignment. But growing, learning, blossoming into true adults is ultimately the most liberating experience we, as women, can hope to attain.

I think it's worth a try.

Epilogue

It would be wonderful if I could write that spending countless hours with the talented women who agreed to be part of *The Self-Confidence Trick* has taught me how to solve all my problems.

Alas, the truth is far less idyllic. I still have an overdraft, my health is less than perfect, Mr Wonderful is nowhere in sight, and I continue to be plagued with sporadic bouts of self-doubt and pointless recrimination.

The moral of the story, then, is that no outside influence – whether it be a man, an excess of money, a friend, or even a book – is capable of doing the hard work of growth for you. They may help and they may provide many of the tools, but the effort is something we have to supply ourselves.

Although the months I spent writing this book didn't result in a trouble-free future for me, it did provide me with several valuable insights. I learned that women who appear to have enviable careers, figures, bank balances, or families have their own problems – and that oftentimes they've had a serious struggle to get to their current 'ideal' lifestyle.

The twenty women you've met between the covers of this book taught me that life can dish out a few unpleasant surprises – Shirley Conran's uncomfortable single motherhood, Emma Nicolson's hearing difficulties, Fay Weldon's fourteen childhood schools, Sally Burton's widowhood, Audrey Slaughter's failure to keep *Working Woman* afloat, the list goes on and on. But women with a vision seem to know instinctively that whatever happens to them can be used to better their life – at some point in the future. They know that just because life is horrid today, it won't necessarily be horrid forever. Our fate – whether good or bad – is not cast in stone; and because it can change we have a responsibility to do our best to change it for the better.

When I began the research for *The Self-Confidence Trick* I wanted to find out what I had in common with 'well-known, achieving' women. Too often I've read about women who have made zillions because they had a better idea, worked longer hours, or approached life with unique talents or gifts. When I thought of these women I felt distanced from them and, unfortunately, inferior. I've never entertained the idea of making zillions, I haven't the stamina or the stubbornness or to work all the hours that God sends, and as anyone who knows me will happily attest, I have no 'unique' talents or gifts. Like most people, I'm blatantly ordinary.

So I wanted to know if successful women, the ones we read about in magazines, see on our TVs, and listen to on the radio might have an ordinary side too. As you've read, they aren't all that different from us after all.

The Self-Confidence Trick is not a recipe for escape into a fantasy world of perpetual pleasure. But it does offer insights into the benefits of coping with adversity – not by running away from it, but by daring to meet life's challenges even when we don't know if we are strong enough to withstand adversity's test. Like the twenty women you've met, you can't help but emerge stronger and wiser – in spite of the scars and bruises.

Several years ago a doctor in California misdiagnosed my symptoms and advised me to go home and get all my affairs in order. His suggestion that my life would end in my thirties at first paralysed me with terror, then suffused me with sadness, and finally resulted in a commitment to make the very most of whatever time was left to me. I'm happy to say that it now seems that my lifespan will be no different from my contemporaries' and that I never did 'get my affairs in order'. Refusing to listen to dictates that strike you as non-productive might be considered stubborn, but to me it makes perfect sense. I'm sure many women who have accomplished things others told them they 'couldn't' do would agree.

If nothing else, I hope that *The Self-Confidence Trick* will encourage you to listen more carefully to the voice within that is, after all, your best guide through life's challenges. When you make friends with the 'inside' you, life becomes less of a struggle and more of an adventure.